Sabotaged by Shame...Now Saved from Shame

SHAME-FREE

Bill & Sue Banks

Distributed   by: Anchor   Ministries
P.O. Box 39
Days Creek,   Oregon   97429
(541)   825-3407

Shame-Free, by Bill & Sue Banks
ISBN # 0-89228-091-3

Copyright, © 2002
    Impact Christian Books, Inc.
    332 Lefingwell Ave.,
    Kirkwood, MO 63122

Cover Design:
    Ideations

Contents

Foreword

There is a remnant of believers in the earth who have a passion to walk in all the liberty which Jesus Christ has given through His life and death, and to help others do the same. Such believers give great segments of their personal time counseling, praying and ministering to folks who reach out to them for help. Bill and Sue Banks are such laborers in these fields so white for harvest.

Out of dedication, determination and love for hurting people come the kind of revelation and help found in this book. Bill called me one day after praying with an individual and asked if the Lord had ever shown me anything about shame. As we talked, I realized he had found another important key in the process of breaking free into full liberty in Christ.

Through Frank and Ida Mae Hammond's revelation about schizophrenia contained in their book, *Pigs in the Parlor,* we had come to know about the deep effects of rejection on the personality, but had not seen the deeper effects of shame. From the beginnings in the Garden, its effects have impacted every individual, knowingly or unknowingly. It is a foundational problem.

I believe everyone, who partakes of the understanding and ministry found in this book, will experience tremendous spiritual and physical benefits and be more able to stand fast in the liberty by which Christ has made them free. Jesus promised, "If the Son therefore shall make you free, ye shall be free indeed." So be it, Lord. So be it!

Thank you, Bill and Sue, for your love for God's people, your faithfulness and steadfastness. The Lord bless you with more revelation, strength, health and love.

A fellow servant,

Stephen Bell
Pastor *Key Ministries,*
Euless, Texas

Introduction

Recently I was asked to write a book about shame, with the goal in mind of helping those suffering from its influences. I hesitated, because I already had three books in the works that I hadn't yet had time to complete. But as the Lord leads we follow, and the very next day I picked up my Bible and it fell open to Psalm 4 where I read:

> O ye sons of men, how long will ye turn my glory
> into **shame**?   Psa. 4:2a

Initially, then, I thought I could write a small pamphlet on the subject, little realizing the full importance of shame in the life of each believer. Since then, I have become amazed at what the Lord has taught and revealed to me about the negative effects of shame. He is so good!

In addition to directing me the very next day to the passage above, the first ministry case that I encountered after deciding to write this book involved *shame*, yet another sign of His leading. And shortly afterwards, I attended a wedding where in the charge to the bride, the minister mentioned that Christ had at the cross exchanged His righteousness for our sin, guilt and *shame*.

This book, therefore, is an answer to that call from the Lord to educate the body about the root of *shame*. I invite you to join me now in discovering the life-changing effects of shame in your life, and the way in which you may become *Shame-Free*.

Bill Banks
Kirkwood, Mo.
March, 2002

Chapter 1

SHAME UNCOVERED

I set out on a search to discover the truth about shame, but it was largely unknown territory. For the most part, I thought, I had been blessed to have been spared shame. In fact, until I began the research for this book, I was unaware of any way that shame had influenced my own life. In retrospect, I realize that I must have been shamed at various points in my life.

As a simple example, something must have occured early on in my life due to a teacher's long forgotten remark. I recall always making it a point to sit as close to the middle of the classroom as I could to avoid notice. If I sat in the front, I would always be called on. If I sat in the back, I would appear to be trying to escape notice and would often get called on. But as long as I sat hidden, in the middle of the class, I was safe. I just blended in. I could still participate, but on my own terms, and when I wished to, by raising my hand.

This method of "hiding in the middle" always seemed to work, although I did not fully realize how truly effective it was until later in life. During my senior year of college I was walking down a hallway with my marketing professor when we met and he introduced me to the professor of Business Law (whose course I had taken the previous year.)

The Law professor politely asked, "You seem like a bright young man, why haven't you taken my Business Law course?"

I responded, "I did, sir, last year."

He seemed puzzled. "Oh really, what grade did you get?"

"An 'A,'" I answered honestly.

He mused, "Then, why don't I remember you?"

Now I knew the reason. I had safely "hidden in the middle."

Empty Hands

Although it would not be considered a conventional experience, my most dramatic encounter with shame happened in 1970, while I lay dying as a terminal cancer patient.[1] It is difficult for me to relate this story even today, thirty years after the fact, without getting choked up.

One evening after spending most of the day on a kidney dialysis machine, I was wheeled to my room in a fit of total exhaustion. I felt as if I had been swimming upstream in the Mississippi all day, and I could barely turn my head and for sure could not lift my arms because of the extreme fatigue. As I waited for someone to move my gurney into my room, I had a conversation with the Lord. I

---

1 The account of the author's miraculous healing from terminal cancer and introduction to the supernatural realm of God's kingdom is related in his book, *Alive Again!* Available from Impact Christian Books.

recall saying (or thinking), "Lord I'm dying and I'm coming home to you."

Suddenly I had the sensation of being in the presence of the Lord, and I realized a shocking truth. I had to admit to Him, "I am coming home to You, Lord, but my hands are empty. I have nothing to bring to You. I have no fruit. Like the 'Littlest Angel' I have nothing to present to You."

I realized at that point that I was a 'fruitless Christian'– I could not point to a single life that I had beneficially influenced for the Lord. The grief that I felt at that moment was almost overwhelming. To this day I am unable to describe sufficiently the sense of shame, embarrassment and grief that I experienced.

Beginning With Scripture: Adam and Eve

And so I began searching for more truth concerning *shame*, and as I did, a larger picture began to emerge. I first looked to the Scriptures for answers, as I usually do: seeking what the Bible had to say about shame, what words were used to describe shame, and what, if any, remedies might be available.

I began by looking at the most obvious case of shame and embarrassment in the Bible – that experienced by our first parents. I turned to the second chapter of Genesis.

*And they were both naked, the man and his wife, and were **not ashamed**.*[2]   Gen. 2:25

---

2 *Strongs* #954. *buwsh, boosh*; a prim. root; prop. to pale, i.e. by impl. to be ashamed...; " See Appendix for complete definitions, and a listing of each Hebrew word used to express variations of shame.

Upon reading this verse again, I was surprised that our first parents were neither ashamed nor embarrassed by their nudity! I had heard numerous explanations for this absence of shame, such as: 'being made in the image of God meant that our first parents were initially covered by a Shekinah-like covering of light or glory.' However, the text indicates clearly that the expected self-reaction to their nudity **should logically have been shame**, or being "ashamed." And yet there was none.

Adam Clarke in commenting upon the nakedness of Adam and Eve, observed: "...shame can only arise from a consciousness of sinful or irregular conduct."[3]

Through the fall, therefore, Adam not only caused mankind to become subject to demons, disease, and death, but also to *shame*! Innocence was lost, and shame was gained.

> And he [Adam] *said, I heard thy voice in the garden, and I was afraid, because I was naked; and I hid myself. And he* [God] *said, Who told thee that thou wast naked?* Gen 3:10-11a

Adam and Eve became fearful of their Father. This is illogical when you consider that God had never done anything unkind to them, and had in fact greatly and lovingly blessed them. And upon fealing this fear, they hid themselves from Him.

Notice their attention became focused upon them-

---

3 *Adam Clarke's Commentary on the Bible.* Baker Book House, Grand Rapids, MI: 1967.

selves for the first time, rather than upon their Wonderful Source and Provider. And immediately they became tormented with shame and self-condemnation. Notice also that Satan, in his first act against mankind, was lazy. He would alway prefer to have us do his work for him: for instance, to condemn ourselves (saving him the effort of accusing us), and even in the extreme, to end our lives (saving him even the effort of trying to arrange an untimely demise).

Adam and Eve were still in the likeness (but no longer in the express image) of God after they had sinned. Apparently their physical bodies had not changed one bit after their rebellion; they had simply lost their covering of the Shekinah-like glory which formerly surrounded them,.

God dwells in unapproachable light (1 Tim. 6:16) and wears it as a covering. Adam and Eve, created in the image and likeness of God, were likewise covered with light, as is their Creator..

> Bless the LORD, O my soul. O LORD my God, thou art very great; thou art clothed with honour and majesty. Who coverest thyself with light as with a garment: who stretchest out the heavens like a curtain:
> Psa 104:1-2

But when they sinned, they lost their covering of righteousness and the corresponding covering of light vanished. They were uncovered, but probably remained unaware of their loss, until it was pointed out to them The word 'naked' would not have existed in their vocabulary, until they heard it from Satan. The Hebrew word rendered 'naked' in the Genesis passage, literally means 'made bare.' When Satan mocked them for their condition, they realized that they had been made bare, that is, that they had lost their covering of light.

Who told thee...? God makes it clear that Adam and Eve would not have come to the conclusion on their own that they were naked, or that their nakedness was shameful, had not someone else (Satan, who still loves to instill shame) made them aware of it.

God's question clearly indicates that shame regarding their bodies was not something that they would have judged on their own. **Their shame was the result of an external, outside judgement, imposed from another source.** Self-consciousness and shame usually result from outside criticism, in the form of the reactions, comments or attitudes of others, or the expectation of those reactions based on previous experiences.

In the Garden, shame entered the scene because of an external judgement to which Adam and Eve were susceptible. They were vulnerable because of their own ingratitude and disobedience to God. But with this vulnerability came the first accusation of Satan, the Accuser of the brethren (Rev. 12:10), and this led to their expectation of both punishment and death for their disobedience.

Why was Satan so eager to shame them (and all their subsequent descendants) and to point out their nakedness? Because he himself had experienced the shame of nakedness. God the Father had stripped from him all his majesty and honor, and removed all the badges of his rank, like a demoted soldier. Consider the pre-fall description of Satan as recorded by Ezekiel, while addressing the King of Tyre, who could not have been in 'the Eden of God':

Son of man, take up a lamentation upon the king of Tyrus, and say unto him, Thus saith the Lord GOD; Thou sealest up the sum, full of wisdom, and perfect in beauty. (12) *Thou hast been in Eden the garden of God; every precious stone was thy covering, the sardius, topaz, and the diamond, the beryl, the onyx, and the jasper, the sapphire, the emerald, and the carbuncle, and gold: the workmanship of thy tabrets and of thy pipes was prepared in thee in the day that thou wast created.* (13) *Thou art the anointed cherub that covereth; and I have set thee so: thou wast upon the holy mountain of God; thou hast walked up and down in the midst of the stones of fire.* (14) *Thou wast perfect in thy ways from the day that thou wast created, till iniquity was found in thee.* (15) *By the multitude of thy merchandise they have filled the midst of thee with violence, and thou hast sinned: therefore I will cast thee as profane out of the mountain of God: and I will destroy thee, O covering cherub, from the midst of the stones of fire.* (16) *Thine heart was lifted up because of thy beauty, thou hast corrupted thy wisdom by reason of thy brightness: I will cast thee to the ground, I will lay thee before kings, that they may behold thee.* (17) *Thou hast defiled thy sanctuaries by the multitude of thine iniquities, by the iniquity of thy traffic; therefore will I bring forth a fire from the midst of thee, it shall devour thee, and I will bring thee to ashes upon the earth in the sight of all them that behold thee.*(18) *All they that know thee among the people shall be **astonished** at thee: thou shalt be a terror, and never shalt thou be any more.* (19)

Ezek. 28:12-19

The word rendered 'astonished' in verse 19 is *Strong's* #8074. *shamem,* which we find frequently translated as 'shame' in the Old Testament, although its primary meaning is "to stupefy, stun, or devastate."

Formerly Satan was clothed with a Shekinah-like glory and splendor that caused him to become prideful . He wasn't able to handle the glory of being in the likeness of God in his pre-fallen state. It corrupted him, and now he hates all those who are in the image of God.. Verse 17 indicates that he was not only blessed with beauty but also with brilliance or brightness (Shekinah glory). He lost all that.

Satan has been now clothed with shame and dishonor. Having been stripped of his beauty, all semblance of the glory of his former covering has been removed. By contrast with his former beauty and splendor, he now stands naked, ugly and undesirable. Thus, it is readily understandable that he would be jealous of God's greatest creation, man; would seek to mock and ridicule those who are 'naked,' and that he would desire to see every living son of God stripped of his righteousness and glorious state (*seated with Christ in the heavenlies* Eph. 2:6).

Satan as he exists today is covered with shame, and

ever since his own fall, his goal has been to instill shame in man, and to accomplish that end, he utilizes all the degrading forms of human activity to bring man to shame, such as drunkenness, perversion, bestiality, and the like.

Previously shame simply did not exist, nor did it need to. As Mark Twain so aptly said, "Man is the only creature that blushes, or who needs to." Since Eden, we continue to experience shame and are in search for a cure. Before the fall, mankind had not experienced shame, even though we were naked. Once we sinned, shame entered the world. Why? Because we disobeyed and failed God, and because someone else (Satan) pointed out to us our loss of a covering.

Shame stemmed from loss of covering, in the same sense that righteousness serves as a covering, and a shield, and offers the protection of God for the believer.

But thou, O LORD, art a shield for me; my glory, and the lifter up of mine head.   Psa. 3:3

We become covered as a new believer with righteousness, and we come under the protection of God. We wear the "armour of righteousness on the right hand and on the left" (2 Cor. 6:7) and our sinful, fleshly nature is covered. Adam and Eve were first covered with righteousness in this sense as well, despite their physical nakedness. After their sin, they were uncovered spiritually and had to replace their righteous covering with a less effective, more mundane covering consisting of animal skins.

In addition, faith is the fuel of righteousness. They experienced a momentary loss of faith in God which went hand-in-hand with their loss of righteous covering, as evidenced when they hid from their loving Father.

I have no doubt that Adam and Eve felt the same sensations which we experience today – their insides shook, mouths became dry, they seemed to be in a mental fog, unable to think...they felt numb, stunned, stupefied, confused, inferior, unworthy, embarrassed...as if all their blood had drained out. They immediately developed a fear of authority, wanted to hide from public view, and somehow felt themselves to be deserving of punishment.

> *And the eyes of them both were opened, and they knew that they were naked; and they sewed fig leaves together, and made themselves aprons.*   Gen. 3:7

We know that Satan is both a "liar" and the "father of lies," but he apparently spoke truthfully when he promised our first parents that they would "know good and evil." Since they already had been immersed in the goodness of God, all they had to "gain" was the **knowledge of evil**. We know today that beauty and ugliness are in the eyes of the beholder, so our first parents' eyes were the first ones enabled to observe and to literally see evil in themselves, where none had existed a moment before.

As we will discover, this area of truth has *sexual overtones* and is in line with the Scriptural definition of shame. Forgive me for speaking bluntly, but we must allow the surgical knife to cut where it must if we are to remove the cancer of shame from our lives.

Apparently their shame was related to their genital areas, *because they made themselves aprons, and not shirts*. The translation brings this thought out as does the Hebrew word utilized: *chagowr, khag-ore,* a belt (for the waist) or apron. (Strongs 2290)

So, clearly there was an association of guilt with their *pudenda*, or external genital areas.

Why, one might ask, should this first couple have felt guilt or been ashamed of their nakedness? Especially since Eve, having been "given in marriage" to Adam by God, was legally, morally and ethically, *his wife*?

Why, indeed? I have wrestled with this question for several years. Because of this research I finally feel that I have found a large part of the answer, and it is related to our present consideration. Each of them suddenly (indubitably with the 'help' of Satan) noticed that they *were different*! Eve did not have something that Adam had, and he realized he had something which differentiated him from her. Psychiatry has referred to a facet of this issue as some form of "envy." However, I feel it is really a matter of *feeling different*.

Much of shame, as we will see, relates to feeling different and in some way inadequate; not as "good" or worthy; not as powerful, intelligent, loveable or acceptable as someone else.

Paul wisely warns us in Second Corinthians not to compare ourselves with our fellowman (or with any of our contemporaries):

19

For we dare not make ourselves of the number, or compare ourselves with some that commend themselves: but they measuring themselves by themselves, and comparing themselves among themselves, are not wise.   2 Cor. 10:12

Comparisons are bound to be a source of difficulty for us. There will always be someone smarter, better-looking, wealthier, or more popular than we are. So automatically, we will be the loser in the comparison, and this then gives the enemy an opportunity to condemn us and to shame us.

We are encouraged in Scripture to come boldly to God's throne in search of grace,

Let us therefore come boldly unto the throne of grace, that we may obtain mercy, and find grace to help in time of need.   Heb. 4:16

It should go without saying, that one cannot come boldly before God, if one is encumbered with t shame, or guilt. This is another reason that it is essential that we deal with our shame.

Things To Come
The following chapters will establish: the biblical basis for shame; the root causes in our personal lives; the (bad) fruit of living with its burden; and finally, the solutions to eradicating this problem. God wants His people free – to be able to serve Him without hindrance, free to

love him and free to love each other in service. May this book help you to so live.

Chapter 2

WHAT IS SHAME?

God has given us the gift of language so that we may be able to classify and differentiate between various ideas and concepts. So what exactly is shame in the language of Scripture?

There are several words translated "shame" in the Bible. The most frequently used word is *"buwsh" or "boosh."* In English, it means simply 'to blush.' It carries with it the thought of humiliation, and represents the feeling of public disgrace, disillusionment, a broken spirit, and being confounded.

Other important Hebrew words dealing with shame include *Kalam, Cherpah, Kana, Shimtash, Shamem, Ervah,* and *Chapher*.

"Kalam" means to wound, taunt, insult with the effect of causing shame, to dishonor or disgrace.

*"Cherpah"*refers to rebuking, pointing the finger, or a stigma.

"Kana" means to cause one to 'bend the knee,' to b r i n g low, to humble.

"*Shimtash*" is 'scornful whispering' (of hostile spectators), to shame.

"*Shamen*" means to cause to grow numb, to devastate.

"*Ervah*" refers to nudity, nakedness, or shame

"*Chapher*" alludes to the detection of the causes of shame.

And thus we have the list of Old Testament Hebrew words for shame. The various New Testament Greek words translated as "shame" really do not add anything new to these Hebrew, Old Testament definitions, the sum of which give a complete picture of Biblical shame.

Along with Scripture, I also verified the meaning of "shame" as defined in modern usage. I reviewed the modern definition according to *Webster's New World Dictionary.*

The first three definitions of **shame** by Webster are particularly relevant to our consideration: "1.) A painful feeling of having lost the respect of others because of improper behavior, incompetence, etc., of one's self or another 2.) a tendency to have feelings of this kind or a capacity for such feelings 3.) dishonor or disgrace (to bring *shame* to one's family)." The College Edition describes it as: "A painful emotion excited by a consciousness of guilt, shortcomings, or impropriety," or "susceptibility to such feeling or emotion."

We might add that shame is an inner sickness, or a 'disease' of the soul, and expresses itself through inner torment. The emotional pain associated with shame comes from what we believe to be true about ourselves – whether it is true or not.

We Need to Differentiate Between Guilt and Shame

As Webster's latter definition associates shame with guilt, we also need to examine the meaning of guilt and its comparison with shame.

Guilt involves a fear of punishment. Shame is certainly related, in that both were present in the Garden after Adam sinned. Both guilt and shame are often linked by their commonly held expectation of punishment or rejection by someone else. However, shame is different than rejection, and differs as well from guilt.

Shame can come from failing to live up to certain standards (real or imagined); guilt results from the breaking of rules.

Shame is rooted in a feeling that we are somehow defective. Guilt is usually related to a mistake that has been made. Shame is obviously worse, because there is no apparent remedy.

Guilt relates to behavior; shame relates to one's very identity.

Guilt entails pain felt for our actions or deeds: shame entails pain felt for our very existence, our personhood, for what is at the core of self, the essence of our being.

Guilt is felt for *making* a mistake: shame is felt for **being a mistake.**

Mistakes I have committed, which caused guilt, can be rectified, but if *I* am defective, how can that be remedied? It seems as if it would require a miracle, as if I would have to be re-created.

Shame also differs from most emotions, in that it is learned, and in many cases initially imposed upon us from without. Although shame begins as an external force, it is soon internalized by the victim and exercised upon his or her being.

Numerous individuals over the past thirty years have passed through my prayer room. Many of them expressed complaints of feeling inadequate or somehow defective, although they rarely used those words. Perhaps it was because they were too tall (or short), too fat (or thin), too busty (or not busty enough), had a nose too long (or too small), a neck too long (or too short), or just the same complaint you have probably heard from your own child at some point, "Nobody likes me." These are all lies of the Devil. Remember the old adage: "God doesn't make junk."

God loves you just as you are. God is the Perfect Gardener and in His wisdom He did not plant exclusively roses or tulips in His Garden. Rather, He placed there a great variety of plants, as it pleased Him. You are, as Isaiah testifies, the planting of the Lord.

*Thy people also shall be all righteous: they shall in-
herit the land for ever, the branch of my planting, the
work of my hands, that I may be glorified.*

Isa. 60:21

*To appoint unto them that mourn in Zion, to give unto
them beauty for ashes, the oil of joy for mourning,
the garment of praise for the spirit of heaviness; that
they might be called trees of righteousness, the planting of the LORD, that he might be glorified.*

Isa. 61:3

So whether you consider yourself a branch or a tree, a
flower or a bush, you are the Lord's planting, that *He might
be glorified*. So glorify Him in, with, and because of your
body. Remember that He has loved you greatly, and has
paid a **great** price for you. And by faith you are made
righteous...a new, beautiful creation in Him.

*For ye are bought with a price: therefore glorify God
in your body, and in your spirit, which are God's.*

1 Cor. 6:20

Through One Man, All Men

Just as Adam's guilt has passed down to all of us, so
has the propensity for shame.

*Wherefore, as by one man sin entered into the world,
and death by sin; and so death passed upon all men,
for that all have sinned:*   Rom. 5:12

Every one of us since the time of Adam has experienced shame or embarrassment, either as a result of our
own actions, or the actions of another with whom we are

identified, such as a child, a spouse or a parent. Later we will discover that shame may also be national, a factor of tribal membership, or due to a society's values and morals.

Shame Can Occur By Association

If you attend a play at your child's school and your child forgets his lines, you feel embarrassed. Why? You sense that it reflects poorly on you somehow. For some reason we take on the shame of our child even though he or she may take it very lightly. If your husband drinks too much at a party and "makes a fool of himself," he may not remember it the next day but you incur shame over his actions. Why? You did not get drunk, but you are shamed because of his actions by association, even if no one mentions it.

Sally's account illustrates this problem of 'shame by association.'

CASE: Sally's Slumber Party

Feelings of shame and inadequacy may be present in spite of a productive and highly successful life, filled with accomplishments. Sally, a well dressed and sophisticated young woman, related her account as we were probing for roots of her demonic fears. She began:

"I was always terribly ashamed of my parents who were both extremely socially inept. They were crude, unable to express love, except to their pets upon whom they lavished excessive affection. I was embarrassed by them and yet instinctively I knew I should not feel the way I felt. I knew I should love and respect my parents. So I was tormented in that area as well. I recall one particularly bad incident in which my father embarrassed me greatly. As little girl of about six, I invited some friends for a sleep-over. Something set my father off and he began to curse like a sailor in front of the girls. I was stunned, as I saw their jaws drop in disbelief. Two of them even called their parents and asked to be picked up, because they no longer wanted to spend the night. I was mortified."

It was little wonder that Sally had problems rooted in her childhood.

Shame Through Others Judging Us

We can be shamed by someone else judging us, either fairly or unfairly. I think many of us have had the experience while in school of standing at the blackboard and attempting unsuccessfully to do some type of mathematic calculation. Very quickly the feelings of ignorance set in, as if the rest of the class could see that we were blushing even through our backs.

Or, continuing to use the school illustration, a teacher might criticize the spelling on a paper we've submitted, or even our handwriting. I can identify with the latter complaint, because I have very often been criticized for my handwriting and admit that my handwriting is so bad, that even I have trouble reading it. (I usually joke that my handwriting is so bad, people have trouble reading my typing).

As a publisher, I have often edited the work of new authors. You can learn quickly in this business whether or not an individual has a teachable spirit. Many times the author is extremely defensive about his work, and some have become so incensed at corrections of their spelling or grammar that they have taken their manuscripts elsewhere.

These authors made a very common error that leads to or results from shame: **they believed that criticism of their work (or performance) was a criticism of them.** They, like so many, mistakenly identified themselves and their sense of worth with their work, job, skill, or strength. And if any of these facets of our functioning are criticized or diminished, we often take it as a personal failure.

The common error is not being able to distinguish between one's self and one's task (or performance, accomplishment, and work). And the hidden truth in the above cases is this: **the enemy planted a lie in the mind of the individuals and each of them believed it.**

Satan's goal is to torment you, to upset you, to deny you rest and peace; to make you feel unloved, unworthy, unacceptable; to prevent you from living the life God intended for you; to get you to question God's goodness towards you (as he did with Adam and Eve); and ultimately to deprive you of life itself. First he tries to prevent your salvation. Having failed at this, he attempts to prevent you from accepting the reality of God's love, from serving God, and from growing into an effective Christian who cares about those around you (e.g to be filled with the knowledge and power of His Holy Spirit). His end goal, should he fail at all these, is to destroy you – to drive you to despair and self-destruction – to cause you to kill part or all of yourself.

We can identify Satan and his area of activity when we put a name to his torment. And then we have taken the important first step to freedom. In order to win the battle we must first know who our enemy really is.

Chapter 3

THE ROOT OF SHAME
IN SCRIPTURE

The following material will highlight the root of shame in the Bible, through various scriptural accounts.

I The Shame of a **People or Nation**, through
    A. The Unrighteous Acts of a Nation
        Seven Causes of Shame Found in Obadiah
    B. The Nation That Mocks God
        Sennacherib Looses Face When He Mocked God
    C. The People Who Persecute God's Anointed
        David Saw Shame Fall on His Persecutors

II. Shame Occurring in **Individual's Lives**, through
    A. Nudity
    B. The Behavior of a Parent
    C. Sexual Assault or Abuse
    D. Unwise Behavior
    E. Laziness
    F. Pride or Haughtiness
    G. Wickedness
    H. Refusal to Receive Instruction or Correction
    I. Presumption
    J. Dishonoring Parents
    K. Gossip and Revealing of Secrets
    L. Sexual Sin

I. THE SHAME OF A PEOPLE OR NATION

Shame can affect an entire nation or people due to a variety of reasons. Three specific cases from the Bible are presented below:

A. The Unrighteous Acts of a Nation - *Seven Causes of Shame Found in Obadiah*

For thy violence against thy brother Jacob **shame**[4] *shall cover thee, and thou shalt be cut off for ever.*

In the day that thou stoodest on the other side, in the day that the strangers carried away captive his forces, and foreigners entered into his gates, and cast lots upon Jerusalem, even thou wast as one of them.

But thou **shouldest not** *have looked on the day of thy brother in the day that he became a stranger;* **neither shouldest** *thou have rejoiced over the children of Judah in the day of their destruction;* **neither shouldest** *thou have spoken proudly in the day of distress.*

Thou **shouldest not** *have entered into the gate of my people in the day of their calamity; yea, thou* **shouldest not** *have looked on their affliction in the day of their calamity, nor have laid hands on their substance in the day of their calamity;*

Neither shouldest *thou have stood in the cross-way, to cut off those of his that did escape;* **neither shouldest** *thou have delivered up those of his that did remain in the day of distress.*

For the day of the LORD is near upon all the heathen: as thou hast done, it shall be done unto thee: thy re-

4 955. *buwshah, boo-shaw'*; fem.; shame

34

ward shall return upon thine own head.

Oba. 1:10-15

Let us consider this awesome warning.

There are seven sins of Esau's descendants enumerated by the Lord, each introduced by *thou shouldest not.* Rather than aiding their kinsmen, the Edomites (as they were known) remained aloof, as if strangers. And even worse, they became active participants in the pillaging of the descendants of Jacob. As verse 10 points out, they were guilty of committing violence against them.

Historically, although Jacob had grievously wronged Esau, Esau had forgiven Jacob. However in this situation, his descendants looked upon his day of trouble as if he (the Israelites) were a stranger. Like those who passed by the injured man in the parable of the Good Samaritan, the Edomites walked on by, even allying themselves with the enemy and committing violence against the decendents of Jacob. When the armies carried away the Israelites and captured God's Holy City, the descendants of Esau did not come to their aid, but instead plundered the Holy City, Jerusalem.

In total, there are seven specific accusations which brought shame:

1. **Denying aid to a brother**
Thou should not have looked...
Edom refused to aid Jacob in his time of trouble, even though kinsmen were obliged by blood to do so, when another kinsman was threatened, or in trouble. (cf Judg. 5:23)

35

2. Rejoicing over another's trouble

They rejoiced...

Edom not only did not aid, but even rejoiced or enjoyed seeing Jacob go down in defeat.

3. Self-righteous judgement of another

They spoke proudly....

They had judged and told others that the Israelites deserved their fate. By their boasting they added insult to injury upon their brothers.

4. Participating in the devastation of another

They entered into the gate of God's people....

Edom was not merely a spectator, but rather became an active participant in the sacking of Jerusalem

5. Taking gain from a brother's trouble

They laid hands on their brother's riches...

And what is worse, "laid their hands on their substance" means they robbed the possession of their brothers by joining in the plundering of the Holy City.

6. Entrapping a brother, Being a stumbling block

They blocked their brothers escape...

At first Edom is charged with looking on, then participating, then blocking the fleeing Israelites from escape...of standing at the crossroads and establishing roadblocks, to prevent the Israelites from successfully fleeing their fallen capital.

7. Denying aid & betraying a fallen brother

They delivered up the Israeli prisoners...

They arrested and handed over the few Israelites who escaped, to serve as slaves. A treacherous, traitorous act.

The sentence of justice by God against Edom is stated in verse 15, *As thou hast done, it shall be done unto thee.* This is a commonly stated principle in Scripture – that the evil which one does to others is brought back upon the head of the perpetrator.

This sentence was fulfilled shortly by the Chaldean invasion which drove Edom out of her own ancient land, forcing her people to move to the west side of the Dead Sea.

National Shame In Our Modern Times

To grasp the truth and significance of verse 15 in the first chapter of Obadiah, '*As thou hast done, it shall be done unto thee,*' we really need to read the 16th chapter of Ezekiel. In Ezekiel, God is preparing the Israelites for judgement because of their mounting sins, and for having broken His covenant.

> *Thou also, which hast judged thy sisters, bear thine own **shame** [dishonor] for thy sins that thou hast committed more abominable than they: they are more righteous than thou: yea, be thou **confounded** [humiliated] also, and bear thy **shame** [dishonor], in that thou hast justified thy sisters.* Ezek. 16:52

We discover a rather frightening similarity between our modern era and this ancient time. In this chapter of Ezekiel, God lays out his case against Jerusalem (as representative of His people) and enumerates their sins.

1. They have played the harlot, committing 'whoredoms.' Spiritual whoredom occurs when an individual, or group, is unfaithful to God and chases after false gods or things of the world, especially false religions or idols.

2. They turned their back on the poor and needy, providing them no help.

3. They have sacrificed their children unto idols.

This third point really jumps out. The Israelites were practicing a more ancient version of what we call abortion today. And the blood of innocents has always had the ear of God; He always hears the cry of innocent blood, and always responds!

God cites a summary point – that they have breached their covenant with Him. He has agreed to be a Husband to Israel, and yet she had been an unfaithful, adulterous wife who cares not for her children. By all standards, this is a damnable charge.

B. The Nation That Mocks God -
Sennacherib Shamed & Defeated

In II Chronicles 32, we find the story of the assault on Israel by Sennacherib, King of Assyria. He taunted and mocked not only Hezekiah, King of Judah, but also God Himself.

> *Now therefore let not Hezekiah deceive you, nor persuade you on this manner, neither yet believe him: for no god of any nation or kingdom was able to deliver his people out of mine hand, and out of the hand of my fathers: how much less shall your God deliver you out of mine hand? And his servants spake yet more against the LORD God, and against his servant Hezekiah. He wrote also letters to rail on the LORD God of Israel, and to speak against him, saying, As the gods of the nations of other lands have not delivered their people out of mine hand, so shall not the God of Hezekiah deliver his people out of mine hand.*
> 2 Chr. 32:10-13

As the account relates, Isaiah cried out to the Lord and the Lord sovereignly cut off the mighty men in the Assyrian camp. We are told that King Sennacherib returned home "with shame of face."

The king of Assyria and his men, who had all mocked God and His chosen people, received their reward from the Lord – shame of face. In the King's specific case, his punishment went beyond mere shame; he suffered death at the hands of his own offspring.

In the cultures of the far east, we are aware that even

today men will go to almost any extreme to avoid losing face, or being shamed. Saving face, or avoiding shame, is a major factor in the culture. In the near East, and the lands of the Bible, it is similarly important to the people to not be shamed. This manifests especially in the area of hospitality.[5]

> *They that hate thee shall be clothed with **shame**;* [blushing] *and the dwelling place of the wicked shall come to nought.* Job 8:22

C. The People Who Persecute God's Anointed -
David Saw Shame Fall on His Persecutors

In a number of Psalms we read of David's battles with his enemies and his cries to God for intervention. In many cases and at various points in time, his enemies sought to shame him; and yet David recognized his place of honor as one of God's anointed. He prayed consistently for the reversal of these attacks.

> *Hear me when I call, O God of my righteousness: thou hast enlarged me when I was in distress; have mercy upon me, and hear my prayer. O ye sons of men, how long will ye turn my glory into **shame**?* [dishonor] *how long will ye love vanity, and seek after leasing?* [lying] *Selah.* Psa. 4:1-2

David's cry to God against His enemies is because they have caused his glory and honor, as one of God's anointed, to be diminished. His enemies have instead loved

5   See the books on covenants by H. C. Trumbull, especially *The Blood Covenant.*

(or perhaps *chosen*) emptiness and have sought falsehood. They apparently had lied ("leasing") about David and attempted to dishonor him.

David proclaims that the righteous who call upon the Lord our God **will not be ashamed**.

> *Let me not be **ashamed**,*[disgraced] *O LORD; for I have called upon thee: let the wicked be **ashamed**,* [humiliated] *and let them be silent in the grave.*
>
> Psa. 31:17

Rather than shame coming upon himself, and by association upon His God, David proclaims that shame is to be sent back upon the enemy of the righteous and their righteous God. And David, through the wisdom and inspiration of the Holy Spirit, then couples *shame* with *death* as the consequence for this attack of dishonor against him (note the similarity with Sennacherib). In the same way David refused to allow Goliath to taunt and shame God's chosen people (and therefore shame God Himself), he now refuses to allow shame to have its place in his own life and defeats it as soundly as he defeated Goliath. A 'bad fruit' which can join itself with shame, therefore, is *death*. Another 'bad fruit' to join shame is *confusion*, as seen below...

> *Let them be confounded and put to **shame*** [dishonor] *that seek after my soul: let them be turned back and brought to confusion that devise my hurt.*
>
> Psa. 35:4

The enemies of David have sought his soul and plotted to cause him adversity, distress, misery, or trouble.

41

Shame and dishonor can cover one like a garment, and both will inflict their hurt and pain upon the sufferer. David's enemies desired to be able to boast that they had destroyed him or 'eaten him up.' David's complaint is that they had rejoiced or been glad when he was in distress, and had been pridefully gleeful over his misfortune.

> *Let them not say in their hearts, Ah, so would we have it: let them not say, We have swallowed him up.Let them be* **ashamed** [caused to blush] *and brought to* **confusion** [shame exposed] *together that rejoice at mine hurt: let them be clothed with* **shame** [blushing] *and* **dishonour** [disgrace] *that magnify themselves against me.*   Psa. 35:25-26

And again, in Psalm 40, David prays for a reversal of the attack of dishonor and shame; that the arrows being sent his way return against the hearts of the senders.

> *Let them be* **ashamed** [caused to blush] *and* **confounded** [dishonored] *together that seek after my soul to destroy it; let them be driven backward and put to* **shame** [taunted with] *that wish me evil. Let them be* **desolate** [devastated] *for a reward of their* **shame** [put to confusion] *that say unto me, Aha, aha.*
>
>   Psa. 40:14-15

The use of the word desolate is significant, for in the Hebrew its meaning is 'to stun, devastate, or stupefy,' (*shamem, shaw-mame).* How often, when embarrassed, do we feel devastated, stunned, stupefied (as well as stupid), and desolate! How often do we feel, as David felt momentarily, abandoned by all his companions and destitute of all help!

The error of his enemies was first and foremost, mocking God's anointed servant and ruler, or anointed authority figure. In particular, they wished, and would have been pleased, for evil to fall upon God's servant. And yet the Lord is continually faithful to his servant David, and rescues him from his enemies.

> *My tongue also shall talk of thy righteousness all the day long: for they are* **confounded**, [public disgrace] *for they are brought unto* **shame**, [exposed to] *that seek my hurt.*   Psa. 71:24

The word rendered shame in Psalm 71 implies detection – bringing to light and fully exposing the shame of his enemies, bringing them reproach. David rejoices and desires to boast of His God, because He has detected (confounded) the enemy and brought shame upon them. Notice that the primary idea of the word rendered shame is detection: to have sins found out, discovered, detected, and uncovered to the shame of the one so exposed.

> *Fill their faces with* **shame**; [disgrace] *that they may seek thy name, O LORD. Let them be* **confounded** [caused to blush] *and troubled for ever; yea, let them be put to* **shame**, [exposed to] *and perish*:
>   Psa. 83:16-17

In the above examples we see that God sends shame upon those who oppose and intend harm for His anointed. The intended shame is returned upon their own heads. And God reveals that an attempt to shame his servant was really an attempt to shame Himself, and He responds accordingly. The error and evil of their attack will become evident, and will be exposed.

II. SHAME OCCURRING IN INDIVIDUAL LIVES

Shame can affect our personal lives in the same way it was shown to affect an entire nation or people. Some of the causes of personal shame in the Bible are presented below:

A. Through Nudity, Exposing Oneself, & Idol Worship

The first occurrence of the term "shame" in the Scripture, following man's exit from the Garden, appears in Exodus when Moses came down from the Mount to find the people worshiping the golden calf.

> *Moses saw that the people were naked; (for Aaron had made them naked unto their **shame** [scornful whispering] among their enemies:)*   Exo. 32:25

The Hebrew word employed is *'shimtsah, shim-tsaw'* meaning scornful whispering of hostile spectators. In addition, the nakedness of the people was an act of idolatrous worship, and this also resulted in shame. Exposing oneself and nudity are characteristics of idolatry and have been associated with false or cultic worship from earliest recorded history.

B. Through Behavior or Action of a Parent

And Saul cast a javelin at him to smite him: whereby Jonathan knew that it was determined of his father to slay David. So Jonathan arose from the table in fierce anger, and did eat no meat the second day of the month: for he was grieved for David, because his fa-

*ther had done him **shame** [an insult].*

1 Sam. 20:33,34

Jonathan became angry and lost his appetite, because his father embarrassed him by breaching the covenant of hospitality and by attacking their guest, his friend, David.

C. Through Sexual Assault or Abuse –
As Revealed in the Account of Tamar

And he said unto him, Why art thou, being the king's son, lean from day to day? wilt thou not tell me? And Amnon said unto him, I love Tamar, my brother Absalom's sister. And Jonadab said unto him, Lay thee down on thy bed, and make thyself sick: and when thy father cometh to see thee, say unto him, I pray thee, let my sister Tamar come, and give me meat, and dress the meat in my sight, that I may see it, and eat it at her hand. So Amnon lay down, and made himself sick: and when the king was come to see him, Amnon said unto the king, I pray thee, let Tamar my sister come, and make me a couple of cakes in my sight, that I may eat at her hand. Then David sent home to Tamar, saying, Go now to thy brother Amnon's house, and dress him meat. So Tamar went to her brother Amnon's house; and he was laid down. And she took flour, and kneaded it, and made cakes in his sight, and did bake the cakes. And she took a pan, and poured them out before him; but he refused to eat. And Amnon said, Have out all men from me. And they went out every man from him. And Amnon said unto Tamar, Bring the meat into the chamber, that I may eat of thine hand. And Tamar took the cakes which she had made, and brought them into the cham-

*ber to Amnon her brother. And when she had brought them unto him to eat, he took hold of her, and said unto her, Come lie with me, my sister. And she answered him, Nay, my brother, do not force me; for no such thing ought to be done in Israel: do not thou this folly. And I, whither shall I cause my **shame** [pointing of the finger, stigma] to go? and as for thee, thou shalt be as one of the fools in Israel. Now therefore, I pray thee, speak unto the king; for he will not withhold me from thee.* 2 Sam. 13:4-13

Tamar tried her best to discourage her brother from raping her, asking in essence, "If you do this thing to me, how could I ever get rid of my shame?"

Today there is forgiveness and hope for all sinners and victims of sin through the blood of Jesus, which will be dealt with more fully in Chapter Seven as we consider Scriptural solutions.

It is interesting to note that the Hebrew word which Tamar used to describe her impending shame includes in its definition the word *pudenda* which refers to the external genital organs of either gender. Once again we discover a sexual connotation involved with a Scriptural word for shame.

D. Through Unwise Behavior

He that reproveth a scorner getteth to himself **shame**:[reproach] *and he that rebuketh a wicked man getteth himself a blot.* Prov. 9:7

Although the intent of the heart of the instructor is right, shame results from trying to correct, or instruct, a

46

scoffer or mocker. We are better advised to direct our efforts to those who will hear our advice and heed it. Similarly, we are admonished to avoid bringing shame upon ourselves by acting unwisely by correcting the wicked who will not hear. Our responsibility is only to tell the truth as a good witness does in court. We are not responsible for the response to our message. Instead of being helpful, we may become the object of derision.

E. Through Laziness

He that gathereth in summer is a wise son: but he that sleepeth in harvest is a son that causeth shame [blushing].   Prov. 10:5

A son, or any man, who sleeps at a time when he should be working, brings shame.

F. Through Pride or Haughtiness

*When pride cometh, then cometh **shame***: [dishonor] *but with the lowly is wisdom.*   Prov. 11:2

We are familiar with another warning in Scripture, that "*Pride goeth before destruction, and an haughty spirit before a fall*" (Prov. 16:18). Or as it is usually quoted, "Pride goeth before a fall." Pride will lead to destruction and to shame, because of a principle which Jesus plainly stated: *...whosoever shall exalt himself shall be abased; and he that shall humble himself shall be exalted.* (Matt. 23:12)

47

G. Through Wickedness

*A righteous man hateth lying: but a wicked man is loathsome, and cometh to **shame*** [detection].

Prov. 13:5

God has repeatedly stated and warned, that the wicked will be covered with shame. "Wickedness" is the Hebrew word *rasha*. It means "morally wrong, godless, lawless, vicious, apostate, oppressor." This term appears more than 265 times in the Old Testament. It is parallel with practically every Hebrew word for sin, evil and iniquity. The wicked cause perpetual agitation in the lives of others and are "guilty of violating the social rights of others through oppression, greed, exploitation, murder, dishonesty in business and twisting of justice."[6]

It is important to understand what is really resulting from wickedness, because wickedness covers a broad range of behavior. The key here is that the wicked person will be the one who is shamed – most likely by those who follow after, or by the onlookers on the day of God's judgment.

H. Through Refusal to Receive Instruction or Correction

*Poverty and **shame*** [dishonor] *shall be to him that refuseth instruction: but he that regardeth reproof shall be honoured.* Prov. 13:18

6. "Lexicon to the Old & New Testaments." *The Hebrew-Greek Key Study Bible.* Edited by Spirios Zodhiates, T.H.D. AMG Publishers, Chattanooga, TN

The one who refuses to accept correction, or teaching, will come to shame and poverty.

I. Through Presumption

*Go not forth hastily to strive, lest thou know not what to do in the end thereof, when thy neighbour hath put thee to **shame*** [disgrace].   Prov. 25:8

*He that answereth a matter before he heareth it, it is folly and **shame*** [reproach] *unto him.*   Prov. 18:13

It has been said, "Nothing can be hated, or loved, until it is first understood." There is also a saying, "Fools rush in, where angels fear to tread." Such is the case of the one who gives an opinion without carefully hearing and considering all of the facts. Hasty judgements can bring humiliation and shame when proven wrong.

J. Through Dishonoring Parents

*He that wasteth his father, and chaseth away his mother, is a son that causeth **shame**,* [blushing] *and bringeth reproach.*   Prov. 19:26

The man who robs his father and drives off his mother, causes shame and reproach. Paul put it this way in Ephesians 6:2-3, *Honour thy father and mother; which is the first commandment with promise; That it may be well with thee, and thou mayest live long on the earth.*

K. Through Gossip and Revealing of Secrets

Debate thy cause with thy neighbour himself; and discover not a secret to another: Lest he that heareth it put thee to **shame,** [forced to bow] *and thine infamy turn not away.*   Prov. 25:9-10

Don't hold a public controversy over matters that should be kept private. 'Neighbor' here could also mean friend, lover or spouse. There is a familiar expression, "Don't air your dirty linen in public." The second admonition is, do not reveal a confidence or secret (the implication of the word is that of being privy to deliberations of a council or assembly.)

As we have seen in this chapter, the Bible shows us that shame is a common consequence which arises from the misdeeds of people. We need to be sensitive to our own shortcomings and eager to repent when the Holy Spirit reveals the need to us. There is, however, a **tormenting root spirit of shame** which victimizes us, tears at us, and wishes to rob us of the fullness of our lives in Jesus Christ. This root spirit is not brought on by our own actions, but as a result of the actions of others against us.

Let us now examine this root of shame which invades our personalities and holds us captive.

Chapter 4

THE ROOT OF SHAME
In Our Lives

Shame, the fear of shame, and the avoidance of shame have probably more to do with shaping our personalities and directing our lives than any other factor.

Traditionally in deliverance circles, **rebellion** and **rejection** have been considered to be the two primary root spirits to be confronted. However, I am beginning to see that there is an even more basic root spirit common in many deliverances – *shame*.[7]

CASE: Tormented Housewife
Shame can literally cripple the individual tormented by its presence. One young housewife whom I used to encounter at various meetings in our area about twenty-five years ago was a victim of shame. Every time the woman saw me she would begin to blush, and tears would course down her cheek. Finally, I asked her why she teared up whenever she saw me. She explained, "Mr. Banks, the reason I cry every time I see you is that I know you can see my sins."

I hastened to assure her that I could not see her sins (nor did I wish to). However, her shame because of them

---

7 Presenting this new area of truth is not to deny the possible influences of a curse nor the reality of other aspects of deliverance. This is merely another tool in our armament against the enemy's wiles.

caused her to feel guilt, embarrassment, and to be fearful that I could see through the exterior veil of her flesh. Her guilt and embarrassment over her known sins were the roots of her shame.

As an interesting parallel, there is an increasing awareness and interest among psychiatrists today regarding the possibility that shame may be a key underlying problem among those with psychological disorders.

What is it that causes someone to **rebel**? Usually, they have encountered a situation in which they were forced to do something which they did not want to do, or which they felt to be beneath their dignity. Similarly, it is this kind of traumatic experience which evokes shame.

Why does a person manifest symptoms of **rejection**? Because he or she has been shamed in some way in the past, quite frequently either by a parent or teacher.

Shame, I also suggest, is also an important root of **depression** and **inferiority**, as well as of rebellion and rejection. Shame says you are defective, no good, and inferior. Thus, your situation is hopeless, and hopelessness by its very nature is depressing.

Shame Can Begin Very Early
There are certain **primary emotions** which are natural and instinctive, such as those associated with pain, discomfort, anger, fear, frustration, love, pleasure, happiness and even joy. These are as natural and instinctive as hunger, thirst, and fatigue. All of the aforementioned emo-

tions, or sensations, are present in a child, even before he or she develops self-awareness. However, there are certain emotions of a secondary category which can only occur after the child becomes aware of self-identity and his or her individuality. These **secondary emotions** include *pride, guilt, embarrassment, shame,* and *self-consciousness*, to cite but a few.

I believe that shame develops in a child even before guilt. Have you ever seen a baby blush? I have, and it was certainly before he was old enough to have grasped the concepts of right and wrong.

Three Possible Sources of Shame

Shame in our personal lives can come from at least three general sources.

First, shame can come from a *perceived failure in our relationship with God* as a result of disobeying His commands, as it did for Adam and Eve.

Any form of sin is an obvious source, or beginning point, for shame. This is one of the reasons many in our society would prefer to believe and teach that there are no absolutes, that there is neither right nor wrong. Such individuals do not want to accept the possibility that there might be a God to whom they will one day be accountable for their actions. They do not want to face the shame for their actions in this life.

Second, shame can come *from man.* Often, shame comes from parents who may create a shame-prone environment by their attitudes and manner of disciplining a child. Parents commonly say, "Shame on you!" and use shame in an attempt to modify or correct behavior, thereby planting the seeds of shame or an expectation of shame.

Another way shame comes from man is through the behavior of parents (or adult guardians) around children. I have ministered to many children and adults also who were ashamed of their parents' indecent sexual behavior: sleeping around, indulging in X-rated movies, and other forms of pornography. It has been surprising to me to hear children of a young age, an age that I would not have expected them to even understand immorality, blushing as they explained to me that they knew about their parents' activities, and that they had been teased because their parents were 'sleeping around.'

Third, shame can also come *from the Devil* who loves to torment and torture individuals with the terrible pain and embarrassment of shame. Since he is a liar, he will arrange embarrassing situations, and even create false guilt, or the impression that we have done something wrong in order to bring shame upon us.[8]

Demonic Doorways for Shame & Other Spirits
Oftentimes shame can develop into demonic proportions. There are three primary ways that an unclean spirit can enter a person:

1. As the result of a traumatic or sinful experience
2. By inheritance
3. As a result of training or teaching.

8. In each case the truths in this book are equally applicable to female victims as to males.

The first two categories are fairly obvious to anyone familiar with deliverance.[9] Trauma and sin open doors for demonic harassment, and some demonic problems are inherited through the family lineage. The third type, however, deserves clarification and the following example will contrast all three methods of entry:

If, for example, you were in an automobile accident, you might pick up a fear either of driving or of auto accidents (#1). If your parent was in an accident before you were conceived, you could inherit a familiar spirit of the fear of being in an auto accident (#2). However, in the case of the third category, you might have been raised by a non-relative who had been in an accident in the past, and every time you were in the car with that person fear was demonstrated. Perhaps you were continually reminded, "Look out for that car, it might hit you!" This form of 'conditioning' can easily develop into a fear of driving, which was a result of being in that fear-ridden environment (#3). In much the same way, one raised by parents who happen to be shame-ridden can also be trained, taught, conditioned to continually be ashamed.

Shame Used for Control
Unfortunately many parents have discovered that shame is an effective tool for exercising control over their children. "If you love me, you will...," "If you are a good son/daughter you will..." In each case the implied alternative, "if you don't..." results in shame.

In a typical situation, a parent disapproves of a child's

9 For further teaching on the subject of deliverance see *Power for Deliverance: Songs of Deliverance* by the same author.

behavior and expresses this to the child implying, or even stating, shame for that behavior. The child, desiring to restore fellowship with the parent(s), changes behavior. However, the child (especially so in the case of older children) gives up a portion of his or her self (soul) to accommodate the parent. This may be true even in instances where a reason for a required change is good and necessary, such as "Don't go out in the street, or I will tell your father."

When a child is shamed by the parent, a soul-tie[10] break occurs and the child feels abandoned. In an effort to reestablish that connection with the parent, the child seeks to restore or win approval by being perfect, or may turn to others to reestablish self-worth. This can lead to a lifetime of dependence, perfectionism, and to continually seeking the approval of others.

On the other hand, shame is considered by some psychologists to be beneficial and instructive, as a means of controlling social behavior. We, however, believe this is never the case. There are better means of correcting behavior. Godly discipline of a child is a form of deliverance. A number of suggestions for ways to discipline are offered in our book, *Deliverance for Children and Teens.*

For instance, being forced to sit in the corner, or wear a 'dunce's cap' at school and 'time-outs' at home, are ways of shaming a child into socially acceptable behavior. Yet each is a form of abandonment and not only shames, but reinforces the feelings of abandonment which may already be present.

10   For further teaching on soul-ties see *Breaking Unhealthy Soul-Ties* by the same authors.

And the one who has been controlled by shame usually will attempt to manipulate others with shame. This is similar to the classic effect of traditional witchcraft in the sense that the one controlled usually winds up controlling others in the same way that he or she was controlled. In much the same way, victims of judgementalism usually become judgemental of others, and will frequently pick up a critical spirit. Such individuals are also often unduly susceptible to and plagued by the comments of others, and can end up depressed and introverted.

Using shame to control behavior is not unlike spiritual witchcraft. Such witchcraft (defined as "manipulation, control, domination"), we have explained in earlier writing as "attempting to get someone to do our will by a power (or spirit) that is not of God."

There is a degree of prostituting one's self in order to gain the acceptance and approval of others. This causes a stifling of the individual's own personality and the assumption of a false personality which does not offend others. Shame is often the reason at the root of this behavior. Think of how much greatness we would demonstrate were we to live in the fullness of our true personality, as God specifically created us!

Shame Through Sexual Abuse

In severe cases, such as those involving sexual abuse of a child, the child dissociates herself or himself, and the true personality is shattered. Shame is introduced by the child's feelings of wrongdoing or failure, and as a means of covering up the sin by the offending party.

CASE: Sexual Abuse #1

During the course of her deliverance, Nancy remembered the occasion of her sexual abuse. She related, "I had the choice of remaining there in the bed with my uncle's sweaty body on top of me and feeling the pain, or getting out of my body. So I chose to remove myself, and I sat across the room on the dresser and just watched. Then when he finished, he threatened me, saying, 'If you tell anyone, you will get blamed; people will hate you, because all of this was your fault.'"

CASE: Sexual Abuse #2

Like most small children, Betty became curious about sex, although at age three or four it was merely about the differences between little boys and little girls. She permitted herself to be led into a shed by an older boy who undressed her. Her memory went no further, but she can still remember the interior of the shed and its moldy smell. This became a source of shame. That caused her in later life to have a knotted stomach and to be terribly anxious about everything. She always expected the worst: envisioning the worst possible dire outcome of every event. If a teenage son was late returning home, she would immediately conclude "He's lying dead in a ditch somewhere."

CASE: Sexual Abuse #3

Henry was a butcher who felt a call of God upon his life. He came to see me because he felt hindered in his walk, and felt that he had to get rid of something before he would be able to answer the call on his life. I sensed that there was something in his past that had caused him great shame, because of his expression, manner and the way he avoided eye contact.

"My father left us when I was two months old, so I never knew him. Mom raised me and worked hard to support us. I know that I have a lot of fears and sexual guilt," he stated. "I have a problem with pornography in particular. And I have absolutely no recollection before age five. Whatever I seem to know about that time frame is what my sister has told me."

Pornography, which is so rampant today, has been, and is, a root of much shame; as are other forms of indecent sexual behavior. As I talked with Henry, I discerned that there was something more than just the longing for a father; there was a fear of homosexuality at work on him. It was evident to me that shame was a strong factor in his life. He had difficulty looking you directly in the eye.

We began ministering deliverance, and casting out the spirits which he felt needed to be dealt with, and the ones I had discerned. Suddenly he said, "Whoa! Wait a minute. I just saw something that the Lord has brought to mind. When I was a small child, just an infant on a bassinet, my mother used to masturbate me. I remember now that she used to do that whenever I cried to quiet me down. She even," and he blushed, "had oral sex with me."

Here was the source of the great shame that had so impacted his life. He repented and renounced his involvement and we commanded the spirit of shame to go. Henry left smiling and rejoicing, looking forward to his new ministry walking in freedom.

CASE: Sexual Abuse #4

Sarah was so burdened with shame that as a child, if home alone and someone knocked at the front door, she would run and hide under her father's desk. Sarah inherited a spirit of shame from her mother, who had been sexually molested by an uncle. Her own sense of shame was regularly reinforced by her mother's continual responses of shame, refusing to mix socially, when at home keeping the shades drawn, etc.

"I had such social fears," Sarah laughed weakly, "If someone came to our home that I didn't know, I'd climb out a window to avoid having to meet them."

Societal Shame

An example of a cultures employing shame as means of control is to be seen in the account in Nathaniel Hawthorne's novel of Hester, who was forced to wear a scarlet letter 'A' as symbol of shame for her act of adultery and bearing a child out of wedlock. The wearing of the scarlet letter was a means of public humiliation and shame. Another practice utilized in early colonial life was the use of public stocks which caused those confined in them to be exposed to ridicule and public humiliation. In much the same way the yellow stars of David which the Jews were forced to wear in Nazi Germany were also badges of shame intended as a mark of humiliation, differentiation and shame.

Our present society facilitates the power and effects of shame through acts of discrimination, by judging certain people or groups to be defective, inferior, or outsiders. Those, so judged, experience shame for non-conformity to the perceived standard. We see this across racial, socio-economic and ethnic lines. Shame, and anger, can also be taught to a child by an adult, who lived through more difficult and turbulent times.

'Color-Shame' is a type of societal shame. God has given me a great compassion and love for all followers of the Lord. Some of this may have been inherited. My mother during her final year had a great many nurses who cared for her and all of them seemed to love her. On one occasion she mentioned that Marcie had brought her a little gift. I asked, "Is Marcy the tall, black nurse?"

She responded, "Why, I really don't know, if she's black or not. I'll have to look the next time she comes in."

What a testimony to her Christian faith and the makeup of her personality. She was literally color-blind where people were concerned.

Many African-Americans have confessed to me in deliverance sessions that they felt shame because of their color. Others have shared with me that they were ashamed for having 'passed' as white. Both of these are tragic to hear and show the deep effects of societal shame. God created all mankind as 'good,' and in His wisdom chose to use varying skin pigmentation, with all his Creation being beautiful to Him.

Others in our society have been taught shame. Some have revealed that their feelings of shame and inferiority relate to their ancestors having been slaves. Often anger and bitterness are present when a person is repeatedly taught about racial abuse. The presence of shame and anger and bitterness can do great harm and stiffle the peace and joy of the Holy Spirit. Love and forgiveness, however, cover a multitude of sins and bring inner freedom.

As an example, I knew a black woman who cleaned houses, and who often remarked that she was treated like a part of the family. However, I learned that she lived in constant fear. Apparently she had been told in her church that the white people hated them and were going to throw dynamite into their church or even into her home. Tragically, she believed what they said. In those days I don't think there was a single case of white-on-black crime in our area. Regrettably some churches and some so-called "ministers" make a living out of exploiting the fears of people. For too long men have made merchandise of the people of God, serving their own ends.

> *In their greed these teachers will exploit you with stories they have made up. Their condemnation has long been hanging over them, and their destruction has not been sleeping.* 2 Pet. 2:3

Regrettably, some people do lump others into stereotyped categories and label them with ethnic slurs. We have grown up in a society where every ethnic group has a stigma or slur of some kind. Perhaps this is the result of the United States being the great metling pot, and develops out of the side-by-side cultural differences still seen today, especially in larger cities. I remember once as a youngster being called an "immigrant" by the local bully. Now I laugh at the prospect of one American calling another American an "immigrant."

There are other shame-causing phrases in our society, such as the labels attached to certain children by their school. Examples include ADD, slow-learner, poor student, or a variety of other words. In addition, there are spoken curses such as, "You'll never learn math," "You'll never be able to hold a job," "You aren't smart enough to go to college," etc. The real tragedy is that the ones so stigmatized will usually believe those lies and thereby limit themselves. And the demonic negativity begins to hamper them from being all they are capable of being.

Comedian George Gobel used to use the line, "I feel like brown shoes in a tuxedo world." Implying that he didn't feel as if he fit in anywhere. Many experiencing shame can identify with that remark.

Social rules and standards cause people to experience shame, but are arbitrary and not universal. For example in certain parts of the world, rather than being embarrassed by burping, to not burp after a meal is considered discourteous and a source of shame for the host.

Families, parents, churches, cultures and societies have all used shame in some way to control the behavior of their members.

CASE: Robert's Societal Shame at Birth
Robert began his account, "Mother conceived me out of wedlock and fleeing from the shame, moved with me to another town where she struggled to support us. Soon she married a man who became my father. Because of her shame and guilt, though, she never told my father and only admitted the circumstances of my birth to me and my

63

brother after my father died. Even after thirty-five years of marriage, she was afraid that my father and his family would reject her."

"I myself have always felt shame and never understood why. I just felt as if there must be something wrong with me and that others could see it, even if I couldn't. You are my last hope. If I don't get help today. I may have to kill myself."

Fortunately, Robert was gloriously set free and left rejoicing.

A Spirit of Shame from the Womb

Some individuals like, Robert, seem to have acquired shame through inheritance and found it to be a part of their personality as far back as they can remember. In Scripture, Jeremiah seems to imply that he, too, had inherited a spirit of shame from the womb:

Wherefore came I forth out of the womb to see labour and sorrow, that my days should be consumed with shame?   Jer. 20:18

CASE: Shame In a Single Parent Home

Tom drove to his college each morning, but spent all day hiding behind the stacks of books in the library until time to go home. He came to see me complaining, "I don't think this is normal behavior." His divorced mother expected him to assume the role of a husband/father substitute. Naturally, he felt inadequate and overwhelm-ed by her expectations, and yet was shamed not only by his inability to meet the need, but also by the perceived inadequacy in his home life as compared to others.

Shame makes a man vulnerable to control by others, especially by those with Jezebel spirits. The evil spirits know exactly where you are vulnerable, and how to find your 'hot button.'

This proved particularly true in Tom's case. Both his mother and grandmother controlled him to the point that when he came to see me, he was virtually incapable of making any decisions on his own. He had a very strong feminine spirit manifesting through him, and feared he might be homosexual, which added to his shame. After confronting his shame and ruthlessly dealing with his demons, eagerly seeking to have them cast out, he was freed. Today he is married with children, and making decisions in life on his own.

The shame-plagued person is insecure – self-confidence is commonly destroyed. Shame devours self-confidence like the roaring lion in Scripture. Shame works hand-in-hand with pride both to 'whipsaw' the individual and to defend its foothold in the personality by preventing any openness to help.

Shame always cripples and hinders the one carrying it. It must be faced, confronted and dealt with, and cast out. If you keep it, it will destroy your very manhood or womanhood, if not take your life.

CASE: Terry & Shame with the Opposite Sex
Terry was a fellow whom I met in college. At some point in his grade school days he had a bad experience attempting to call a girl on the phone. As a result of the shame that he experienced, he could not, and absolutely

refused to, call a girl on the phone. It became a virtual phobia for him. When it came time to try to get a date for a college dance or other function, he would have to have someone else set him up. On very rare occasions he would manage to find a girl whom he could ask in person, which was difficult because he was so shy. To this day he remains single, into his sixties – all because his personality was shaped by a grade school shaming experience.

Embarrassing Situations Don't Always Cause Shame

Shame differs from embarrassment in that embarrassment is usually the result of some action or mistake which is considered to be relatively unimportant, and outside oneself. For example, if I spill my beverage at a dinner party, I am embarrassed by my clumsiness, but my self-worth is not threatened. This has a lot to do however with one's personality and how one was raised. If you were raised in a home that taught you not to take yourself too seriously, you will probably be better able to avoid shame. If however, you have a spirit of shame already in place, the embarrassment of the spilled beverage can be disastrous.

Summary

When shame is left unconfronted, it can produce rotten fruit not only in our lives, but in the lives of those around us. By examining some of this fruit, we should become even more determined to pull this root spirit out of our souls.

Chapter 5

THE FRUIT OF SHAME
In Our Lives

I have discovered that shame, like faith, can function both as a **root** and as a **fruit**. As an example, if you feel shame over being born out of wedlock, you may lie to cover up this fact. You may avoid shame by telling others that you have a wonderful, loving father. Satan, being the father of lies, loves this kind of reaction but then turns around and hits you with guilt and condemnation because you have lied. This double-whammy effect of Satan's torment I call 'whipsawing' and we will consider this in detail a little later.

We have been considering shame as a root problem, but clearly shame bears rotten fruit.

Differing Personal Responses to Shame
Why does one individual experience shame more easily than another? People differ in their responses and reactions to situations. For example twin sons might be born into a loving family, be raised in essentially identical environmental situations, yet one be shame prone and the other not. Why? Because people differ in reaction even to identical stimuli. As an illustration, consider a potato and an egg. If we place each of them in the identical environment of hot water, the egg becomes hard and the potato soft. Why? The situation was the same for each of them,

but because of inner differences the outcomes were quite different.

No two people have had exactly the same backgrounds. Some have been unfairly punished, treated unjustly, or feel that they have, and so their reactions to being treated unfairly in the future may be much more painful and felt more deeply. In the same sense, some people are hardened by their painful experience while others instead become timid or fearful. Rejection may cause one person to withdraw and feel guilty as if he deserved the rejection, while another will simply become angry.

We also tend to experience shame when we feel that our performance is not up to our own personal standard, which may be exclusive to you. As an example, my dad was in the shoe business and always noticed the shine (or lack thereof) on people's shoes. So I tend to be somewhat embarrassed if my shoes aren't properly shined, which they often aren't. However, unshined shoes may not bother you at all.

Bad Fruit #1
Shame Affects Mental Function
People experiencing shame tend to shut down mentally, much like someone who is drunk, and they have difficulty accepting or processing what you say to them (such as, "You shouldn't be embarrassed about that..."). Such intentionally helpful advice does no more good than trying to tell someone who is hungry not to think about food, or to someone experiencing an attack of irrational fear that there is nothing to fear.

Bad Fruit #2
Shame Isolates

Shame disconnects us from other people, even from God, as it did for Adam and Eve. The person feels isolated and is shut-off from everyone, which is a typical technique of the enemy. Or better put, the victim shuts himself off from everyone who might be able to offer help, or from those who at least could offer support and acceptance.

A person who has experienced shame in a particular area of his life does not want to have to experience the discomfort or pain of that traumatic occurrence again, so he buries it. He wants to keep that source of shame a secret and often attempts to cover up the shame with diversions, which may include outbursts of rage when there is a threat that the secret shame might be exposed. If the root is identified or threatened, the victim lashes out in what appears to be an offensive rage, but what is in reality a defensive response. Rage like shame is all encompassing. It can also literally take over a person. And that individual then becomes oblivious to everything else.

Shame isolates an individual and causes him to question his self-worth. It becomes almost like a form of paranoia – "Everyone will hate me for what I have done (or said)." The person enters a black hole. As I have often observed, "Fear and mushrooms grow in the dark." So long as the shame is felt, and permitted its requisite secrecy, it grows and festers. Bringing the light of the Holy Spirit to bear upon it, by sharing it with a prayer partner or a minister and exposing the issue to prayer (or sometimes merely to the light of day, by simply sharing it) can bring freedom. The light dispels the darkness of the shame and its attendant fear.

Bad Fruit #3
Shame Can Destroy Spiritually and Physically

Shame is a spiritual issue. We know this because all of its manifestations lead in some way to self-destructive behavior. The victim feels somehow undeserving or unworthy of life, which can be a precursor to 'spiritual' suicide. Since these individuals feel cut off, estranged even from God by their perceived defects, they begin to die spiritually. A spiritual effect always has a physical counterpart, and spiritual death corresponds to physical death. Thus in more severe cases, the shame-sufferer begins a journey towards 'physical' suicide unless loving intervention occurs.

Shame can be extremely destructive. I believe it was shame in most (if not all) of the cases of individuals who lost their funds and then committed suicide in the Great Depression. They were shamed by the prospect of having to admit to family, friends, and associates that they were broke, or shamed that they had somehow been foolish with their investments, or shamed to be identified with those who live in poverty.

Shame is a very powerful tool used effectively by the enemy of our souls to destroy. Shame works silently from within like a cancer, or fifth column, to bring us to spiritual, if not actual, suicide. Shame thus brings with it related spirits such as depression and suicide. We will learn more about related spirits in Chapter 6. Because the sufferer feels inadequate and defective, he or she becomes depressed. Depression, in much the same way, is a form of destruction of the soul and similarly results, if unchecked, in a spiritual suicide of the soul.

Bad Fruit #4
Shame Can Cause Mental Instability

Shame also can literally bring one to the point of mental instability. The destructive voices crowd out the positive affirmations in our innermost being. The story of Jack illustrates this point.

CASE: Jack Shamed Into Mental Breakdown

I discovered this with the case of Jack, a man accused (falsely) by the Internal Revenue Service of cheating on his income tax by understating his income. He told me that he had in fact, "Always overpaid taxes, rather than to take any chances." He was a man whose self-identity was closely tied to his wealth. When the IRS served him a subpoena for his records and sent a letter threatening to take his home, impound his business, etc. (not once, but several times), he wound up in a mental ward, requiring shock treatments. It was shame that drove him to that point.

While undergoing that shame attack, he was similar to a drug addict or alcoholic; he could talk of nothing else. He became obsessed with what others were saying or thinking about him, approaching an almost terminal embarrassment. He was completely absorbed with his shame, and was unable to receive or process any positive information, although he was actually very intelligent.

This is illustrative of commonly observed effects of shame: obsession and perfectionism. Often the sufferer becomes obsessed with a problem, and tries in his or her own effort alone to never fall prey to shame in this area again.

Bad Fruit #5
Shame Leads to Explosive Personalities
The shame-tormented individual will commonly employ an explosive personality defense mechanism in an attempt to control his environment and to protect his area of shame from exposure. Common defense mechanisms employed by such individuals may include outbursts of rage, as well as diversions of many varieties such as lying, or in general doing anything to divert attention from the area of hurt or shame. The individual is afraid to look at himself honestly, and therefore avoids doing so at all costs.

Bad Fruit #6
Shame Leads to Social Phobia
In social situations, a shamed person may feel so different from what he or she perceives to be the life experiences of "normal" people that they lock-up in interactions with others. This results in what is called a "social phobia" – nervousness around others – a fear that if the 'real you' were to be found out, more shame and rejection would occur.

CASE: Barry's Physical Appearance, and His Social Phobia
Barry was a high school senior who wrote me a heart-wrenching letter describing how his life had been ruined

because he had been born with a nose that was too long. He said he was too ashamed to be seen in public, wouldn't date, hated to have to attend classes at high school, etc. He literally felt that he was defective, and shamed by his disfigurement. He even sent a picture to illustrate his problem. His nose was slightly longer than some, but he was not the freak of nature that the Devil had been telling him that he was.

I wrote him and told him that to me he looked fine, and hopefully offered a little comfort and counsel.

Bad Fruit #7
Shame Causes Self-Focusing

As with Barry, shame is particularly diabolical in that it focuses upon the self, causing the victim to become extremely self-centered. Yet, at the same time, it also seeks to destroy the self by isolating it from all others (even from God!). Individuals prone to shame tend to be extremely self-focused. The person who is either entirely, or primarily, self-focused is totally absorbed with his or her own issues and problems. So much so in fact, that a relatively minor problem such as losing car keys gets blown way out of proportion. When this sudden and public raging subsides, he or she will try to be invisible, to escape or hide, and will be found beating himself up for weeks over the perceived failure. Why? Because the shame and abandonment-plagued individual feels this is another proof of his lack of worth. It is another failure to attain perfection. Any perceived failure is a source of self-shame, causing anger, fear and torment. You may frequently hear such individuals say, "I hate myself."

Bad Fruit #8
Over-Analyzing the Root of Shame

Another facet seen regularly by those ministering deliverance is that shamed-individuals want to consistently over-analyze their actions or motivations. This is most frequently seen among those who have had sessions with psychologists. When they come for deliverance, they expect to spend hours discussing their symptoms, which can be the Devil's stalling tactic against actually commencing ministry. They often want to scrupulously search for hidden motivations (more often natural, rather than spiritual). They have struggled for so long trying to understand why they feel so inadequate and different that the need for this understanding has become an obsession in itself.

Bad Fruit #9
Shame Leads to Disassociation

With shame comes a commonly observed defense mechanism: disassociation. When disassociation occurs, there is a shutting down of our God-given inner reassuring, and a shutting out of everything else, especially those experiences which are too painful for the individual to consciously bear (such as a child undergoing sexual abuse, witnessing a murder, seeing a loved one burned to death, etc.)

Disassociation, disconnecting, blanking, or black-ing-out may occur when a child is sexually abused, or when certain life experiences are considered too painful to accept, or when memories are just too painful to be faced or retained. The mind of the person tries to simply blank out the memory. Not only is the person unable to remember much of what occurred, but certain situations in their life recall the pain of the initial source of shame, and these too are blacked-out. There is a similar effect to that of shock treatment, where entire segments of one's life may be blanked out of memory. Or, at least until they are loving restored and healed by one praying the individual through to victory. The person dissociates himself from the past, and abandons the present painful situation.

Bad Fruit #10
Emotional Starvation and Addictions

The shame-tormented individual is emotionally starved by the effects of shame, suffering from a condition much like emotional anorexia. Like that other wasting disease, if allowed to fully run its course, shame will destroy its victim, because the individual is isolated from healthy, human contact by his torments. He is like a drowning victim gasping for air, and seeks to find a means of fulfilling the tremendous void created by the shame, or to find a way to escape from it. The result is all too often is to fall into an **addiction**.

There are three categories of addiction which are shame related and which consistently repeat the whipsawing cycle: *Alcoholism, Perfectionism* and *Work-a-holism.*

Alcoholism

We consider alcoholism first because it is perhaps the most common and the most obvious. The tormented individual will frequently turn to drugs, drink and sex in attempts to hide or escape from the painful reality of his shame.

CASE: Joe & His Deliverance from Alcoholism

Joe came to see me years ago. Standing across the counter from me in our bookstore, breathing his 80 proof breath on me, he slurred, "I've heard you can help me. I need deliverance, because I'm an alcoholic."

I knew he was still drunk, and not ready to be delivered, so I simply told him, "You're drunk now and are not ready for deliverance, but let me pray for you." I then proceeded to pray that God would bring him to his senses, make him serious about getting free from alcohol, and keep him safe until he could be delivered. He slurred out a "Thanks" and left. I didn't see him for about a year and then he came into our store again. "Mr. Banks," he began hesitatingly, "I don't know if you will remember me, but I came here almost a year ago and asked you to pray for my deliverance. You prayed for me that day, and I can't remember a single word that you said – but I could tell that you believed every word. Now I am back again, and I'm sober this time."

After an hour of confessing and forgiving those who had hurt and shamed him in the past, he was set free.

The alcoholic is burdened with shame, despair, self-hate and disgust. Yet it is often difficult to determine whether we are dealing with the root or the fruit: whether the person drinks because of shame or is shamed because of drinking. My sense is that there is always a root of shame present with alcoholism. There may, for instance, be a sense that his wife doesn't really love him, that he is not the proper head of his family, that he has failed God, that there is some sin in his past that he can't get over. Or perhaps there is just a vague emptiness from a lack of an adequate relationship with a parent. Shame is consistently the root in all these cases.

More specifically, alcoholics often suffer from a lack of relationship with a father-figure. Many adult males testify of their lifelong search for a father. Never being able to find a father, to win the love and acceptance of a father-figure, or to live up to some stated, implied or perceived standard, gives them a reason (or excuse) for drinking.

Many alcoholics are intimidated by men. The lack of a father-figure can cause one of two extremes: to develop a fear of men, or to develop an unhealthy need for a relationship with an older male. This in turn develops a fear of, or vulnerability toward, homosexuality. Many feel that they are in some way inadequate as males – again related to the lack of a clear father-figure and mentor.

Alcoholics usually have marital difficulties, and divorce is a very common result of alcoholism.

Feeling different, or being made to feel different, is a major tool employed by the enemy to isolate and torment individuals. He plays upon the vulnerability of the victim to tell them that no one likes them, or loves them, or that they are abnormal, or even homosexual. This vague feeling of not being fulfilled in manhood, or fear of homosexuality (although rarely acted upon), causes many to be extremely angry and violent when drunk. Have you ever noticed how many intoxicated men want to fight, prove their sexual prowess or attempt some dangerous stunt when they are drinking?

Perfectionism

It is evident that both children and adults may be perfectionists. The shame-ridden adult, like the child, is driven to attain perfection in an attempt to win approval from various sources: parents, or a distant entity to them, like God, or an absent parent (living or dead), or even an ex-mate. Sometimes it is an authority figure from the past who has shamed the sufferer. Whatever the source of shame, the individual simply knows that he must do better, in fact *be perfect*, if he is to be accepted. The standard he is trying to attain may be entirely of his own creation, but has at its core the winning of approval, and becomes a major force in his life.

As we have observed, the standards we set for ourselves are often impossible to attain. This is especially true for those standards imposed on us from our past. We cannot change the past, no matter how hard we try or may work at it.

Work-a-holism

The work-a-holic, like the drug addict or alcoholic, is attempting to compensate for the void which shame has created in his life by working harder. He, too, is working in an attempt to win approval of someone, to be a success among his peers, to prove himself to someone (boss, contemporaries, family, parents, etc.). Instead of escaping into alcohol, he escapes into his work. His job becomes his 'mistress.' As noted, the alcoholic justifies his drinking for negative reasons, "because someone has mistreated me." The work-a-holic, however, justifies his over-working for positive, even noble reasons, "I am working hard to

78

support my family;' 'We need the money;' 'I have to get ahead,' etc. He seeks to justify his worthiness by working, although somewhere down deep he realizes that he is paying too high a price for acceptance. This high price includes sacrificing his family life, and sometimes even his family.

Tragically, many men have tried to find escape via addictions, lust, pornography, sex (including telephone & Internet), food, alcohol, drugs, or to prove themselves through perfectionism or working harder – all in an attempt to hide or escape from the painful reality of their shame. Yet all of these avenues have only served to increase their shame and the whipsaw of their torment.

The Full Picture

Before we get to the solution, it is important to see the entire picture. Shame has related or 'associate' spirits. **In fact it is these related spirits which we usually see first in ourselves and others,** and shame is hiding close by in the shadows. We need to recognize that these branches and limbs grow from the root of shame in our lives. In doing so, we expose this powerful root to the light of day.

Chapter 6

ASSOCIATES OF SHAME
Spirits That Enter Because
of the Root of Shame

A. Spirits of Inferiority

B. Spirits of Self-Protection and Control

C. Spirits of Rebellion and Anger

D. Spirits of Competition

E. Spirits of Rejection

F. Spirits of Self-Focus

G. Spirits of Social Fear

H. Spirits of Sexual Guilt

I. Spirits of Other Types of Fears

Familiar Spirits

In the previous chapters, numerous familiar (or 'family') spirits of shame have been identified. Most commonly they have related to sins of parents or ancestors, (such as incest-shame, alcoholism-shame, adultery-shame).

This chapter will cover nine categories of spirits which can emerge from a root-sprit of shame.

The following is not intended as a complete list of every possible kind of spirit or problem resulting from, or causal to, shame. However the list will be helpful in pinpointing areas where you may have been attacked, perhaps without even being aware of what was at work.

LIST OF SPIRITS WHICH MAY BE INVOLVED WITH, OR ROOTED IN, SHAME

A. Spirits of Inferiority

Condemnation
Confusion
Embarrassment
Inadequacy
Incompetence
Shyness
Unworthiness

B. Spirits of Self-Protection & Control

Ego
Pride
Vanity
Self-righteousness
Haughtiness
Importance
Arrogance
Perfection (ism)
Manipulation

Spirits of pride and vanity might seem to be out of place in this list of shame spirits, however one must understand how evil spirits operate. Demons tend to whipsaw the tormented individual. With regard to shame, a person can be tormented with shame and yet inwardly be hearing pride speaking, "I don't deserve to be treated like this. I am better than those people who are criticizing me, or looking down on me, because I am... smarter, better educated, more religious, etc." And often a proud, unteachable-spirit develops.

Any desire for the the ability to control others or to manipulate others in order to compensate for feelings of inferiority, can lead to involvement in cults or the occult.[1] As Paul writes in Ephesians:

11. For further information on spiritual bondages which come from cults and the occult, see Derek Prince's *They Shall Expel Demons*, Baker Books 1998, and visit our website *www.impactchristianbooks.com* and search under "occult."

And have no fellowship with the unfruitful works of darkness, but rather reprove them. For it is a shame even to speak of those things which are done of them in secret. Eph. 5:11-12

Involvement with the occult brings a whole separate list of spiritual issues and curses. And we are told in Samuel that even rebellion is as the sin of witchcraft (see below).

C. Spirits of Rebellion and Anger

Criticism
Frustration
Irritability
Intolerance
Resentment

D. Spirits of Competition

Our own natures want to be the best, the most loved, or the most deserving of acceptance. This category would be similar to the self-protective spirits, and would include spirits such as:

Envy
Jealousy
Competition
Comparison

E. Spirits of Rejection

Self-rejection

Self-condemnation
Feeling Unloved
Feeling Unwanted
Feeling Unaccepted
Abandonment

As indicated previously, demons tend to *whipsaw* the individual hosting them. A demon lusts to have its nature manifested. If I have a spirit of rejection, merely having it doesn't give it an opportunity to fulfill its lust to be rejected. Something must occur to cause rejection, for it to feed upon. So what usually happens is that the spirit of rejection invites along with it a 'rejection-causing' spirit and they together work hand-in-hand.

The rejection-causing demon has me say to you something like, "Wow, someone with your build shouldn't wear plaid." Even if you do not dignify my comment with a response, the demon can say to me, "Did you see that look? That person thinks you are just as stupid as I have been telling you that you are. You really are no good."

A child may begin to lie, or tell half-truths, to avoid answering the questions of a parent, especially when the child anticipates that the parent will react negatively (or that the answer will result in shame and rejection).

Some fear that they will be abandoned if they are not perfect. The fear of abandonment is activated when one feels he has been discovered to be defective, inadequate, or not up to the standard. That shame-plagued individual believes that either a particular individual, or everyone in general, can see nothing good in them, and that all eyes are on their self-perceived flaw. [12]

This then becomes an all-consuming issue in his or her life, and causes the individual to seek to hide, conceal, isolate, and avoid any further chance of exposure of that painful splinter of inadequacy. A form of terror is experienced by those fearing abandonment.

There is in fact a close connection between shame and the fear of abandonment. Both, for instance, concern an expectation or fear that a person is going to be rejected – often for some reason that he or she cannot understand. There is usually a vague feeling of dread, which can quickly become a panic. This kind of fear seems to be totally irrational.

As with shame, abandonment may either be due to a rational or an irrational fear. Certainly all fear is irrational to some degree for Christians. In speaking of the rational aspect of the fear of abandonment, I refer to a fear based upon an actual fact in the victim's history, such as actually being abandoned by the parents, the death of a parent, or a similar traumatic event which created an expectancy of being abandoned. However, sometimes this fear may be irrational; the victim is unable to recall any type of precipitating event, or years of inward scrutiny have blown an event out of proportion. The most puzzling cases are those where the person happens to be both physically and socially attractive; there is nothing "wrong" with them in

12. For more information on the spirit of abandonment, see the author's other books, *Deliverance for Children and Teens, Songs of Deliverance*.

superficial terms; there seems to be no basis at all for the fear. [13]

However, if I am a victim of a shame-related fear of abandonment, I feel that I deserve to be abandoned, because in my mind, *I am defective.*

F. Spirits of Self: Self-focused Spirits

Demons, as well as your own flesh, want to keep the entire focus of your life on *you.* The more *self-focused* you are, the less *God-focused* you can be, and the less ministry you can have in the lives of others.

> Self-awareness
> Self-consciousness
> Over-sensitivity
> Regret
> Self-Reproach

G. Spirits of Social Fear

> Blushing
> Confusion
> Ill-at-ease
> Incoherence
> Forgetfulness
> Mind going blank
> Perspiration
> Mortified
> Stuttering

13. This is where good (deliverance) detective work is needed to find the source of the fear.

H. Spirits of Sexual Guilt

Abortion
Adultery
Bestiality
Early Sexual Experimentation
Fornication
Homosexuality/Lesbianism
Incest
Lust
Fantasy Lust
Masturbation
Molestation
Pornography

I. Spirits of Fear

Fear of Humiliation
Fear of Appearing Stupid
Fear of Being Called upon in Public
Fear of Being the Center of Attention
Fear of Being Made a Spectacle
Fear of Disgrace
Fear of Inferiority & Inferiority
Fear of Inadequacy
Fear of Incompetence
Fear of Rejection
Fear of Making a Fool of Oneself
Fear of Man
Fear of Condemnation
Fear of Criticism
Fear of Failing God

Fear of Embarrassment
Fear of Failure
Fear of Disappointment
Fear of Disapproval
Fear of Accusation
Fear of Dying (of embarrassment)
Fear of Loss of Respect
Fear of Loss of Reputation
Fear of Public-Speaking

In a recent national secular survey, public-speaking was cited as most people's *number one* fear.

Summary

It is very clear that shame is a root problem which carries with it other harmful spirits. Working together with these spirits, this root spirit seeks to push an individual's personality out of balance. But what can be done to save the sufferer from the grips of shame?

Chapter 7

SCRIPTURAL SOLUTIONS FOR SHAME

It is important to observe that after Adam and Eve fell, God Himself covered them, so that no portion of their beings was any longer legitimately exposed to the accusations of Satan. If the covering which God provided for Adam and Eve was adequate, then how much more sufficient is our *better* covering with the blood of Jesus. Satan no longer has any right to condemn us, once we are partakers of, and covered with, the righteousness of Jesus.

Even more significant from a New Testament perspective, we are comforted by the fact that Jesus Christ personally experienced shame, and therefore, under-stands our suffering.

> *I gave my back to the smiters, and my cheeks to them that plucked off the hair: I hid not my face from shame* [disgrace] *and spitting. For the Lord GOD will help me; therefore shall I not be confounded* [dishonored]: *therefore have I set my face like a flint, and I know that I shall not be ashamed* [caused to blush].
>
> Isa. 50:6-7

Jesus made a willful choice to accept His death 'at the hands of sinful men' without a word of complaint. He willfully determined not to hide Himself from shame or spitting, as He easily could have done. Rather, He chose to pay the price in full for shame, just as He did for sin and sickness. To be freed from shame, we must make Jesus our focus.

> *Looking unto Jesus the author and finisher of our faith; who for the joy that was set before him endured the cross, despising the* **shame***,* [perceived disgrace] *and is set down at the right hand of the throne of God.*   Heb. 12:2

Jesus believed in the love of God His Father, and that God had a good plan in store for Him, as should every believer. He did not, therefore, shrink back from the shame of dying a criminal's death upon the cross. Instead, He continued obeying God to the best of His ability. As *Wilson's* translation renders it, He "dis-regarded the shame." We should do likewise.

Jesus *rejected* His rejection, and *despised* His shame. As various translators have rendered this verse: "looked with contempt upon its shame" (*Weymouth*), "thought nothing of its shame" (*Moffat*), "cared nothing for.." (*Goodspeed*), "was heedless of ..." (*TCNT*), "made light of its disgrace" (*New English*), and "scorned its shame" (*Norlie*).

That the bearing of shame was an integral part of Jesus's crucifixion is to be seen in Hebrews 6:6 which speaks of Christ's shame in a warning. This verse warns that if one should fall away after having the full knowledge and acceptance of all Jesus was, and all that He accomplished on the cross, it would be impossible to renew them again "to repentance." They would have to re-crucify the Son of God, and "put Him [again] to open shame."

The Greek word employed here is *paradeig-matizo* which carries the thought of Christ being made a public spectacle exposed to infamy, openly shamed.

Jesus, you recall, *made Himself of no reputation;* He willing chose obedience to God over personal dignity. This is also a characteristic we would do well to emulate. After all, if God is for me, what can man do to me? (Psa. 118:6). The only person whom I need to please in this life is God! Therefore I need not fear, nor be overly concerned with, man's opinion of me.

Jesus was cruelly shamed and mocked upon the cross where He bore our shame and paid for the nakedness of Adam as well as our own.

> *Then the soldiers of the governor took Jesus into the common hall, and gathered unto him the whole band of soldiers. And they stripped him, and put on him a scarlet robe. And when they had platted a crown of thorns, they put it upon his head, and a reed in his right hand: and they bowed the knee before him, and mocked him, saying, Hail, King of the Jews! And they spit upon him, and took the reed, and smote him on the head. And after that they had mocked him, they took the robe off from him, and put his own raiment on him, and led him away to crucify him.*
>
> *And they crucified him, and parted his garments, casting lots: that it might be fulfilled which was spoken by the prophet, They parted my garments among them, and upon my vesture did they cast lots.* Mat. 27:27-31,35

Although they mocked Jesus and put a robe of scarlet upon him (reminiscent of the shame associated with the scarlet letter mentioned earlier) Jesus was unjustly accused and they could find no sin in Him. Because He already wore, in the spirit realm, a white robe of righteousness. We are also reminded that God has promised that though our sin be as scarlet, they shall be as white as snow.

Notice the complete perfection of God's provision for shame: Jesus was stripped naked and exposed to public humiliation three times prior to His actual crucifixion. The soldiers stripped Him twice, once to put on the robe of mockery and then after they had abused Him shamefully, they removed that robe to replace His own clothing. He was them stripped again a third time in preparation for the cross, when they took His garments to gamble for them The crucifixion was itself not merely a means of execution, but also a means of public shame, as evidenced by the nakedness, the placement of the crosses near the crossroads where all travelers could see the victims So public and universal was the shame which Jesus bore that it had to be labeled in three languages.

One must not, however, miss the obvious truth of all these verses: **Jesus bore *our shame* upon the cross**. He did a completely complete, and perfectly perfect, work. Without complaint, He bore *His* shame and disgrace as well as *our* shame and disgrace, even to the point of suffering as a common criminal and dying a criminal's death. He bore the personal shame and disgrace of having his naked, scarred, bleeding body elevated on public display and mocked, beside a public thoroughfare. Do not be misled by the sanitized artwork we are familiar with today.

94

This was not a comfortable scene as He hung upon the cross – He was naked and broken, without a strip of clothing to cover Him.

No matter what shame, disgrace or embarrassment you feel you have undergone, Jesus not only understands, but has already borne it and made provision for your healing and deliverance! He has already clearly expressed His will for you to be freed from every vestige of shame, in exactly the same way that He has expressed His will for you to be freed from every sin and every sickness – by His substitutional death upon the cross. He willingly died to pay the full price for all your sins, for all your guilt, for all your sicknesses and **for all your shame!**

Remember these powerful words of promise:

*But if we walk in the light, as he is in the light, we have fellowship one with another, and **the blood of Jesus Christ** his Son **cleanseth us from all sin**.*
1 John 1:7

So that,

*There is therefore **now no condemnation** to them which are in Christ Jesus, who walk not after the flesh, but after the Spirit.*   Rom. 8:1

GOD'S PROMISE TO REMOVE SHAME

*Fear not; for thou shalt not be **ashamed*** [caused to blush]: *neither be thou confounded; for thou shalt not be put to **shame*** [not detected]: *for thou shalt forget the **shame*** [confusion] *of thy youth, and shalt not remember the reproach of thy widowhood any more. For thy Maker is thine husband; the LORD of hosts is his name; and thy Redeemer the Holy One of Israel; The God of the whole earth shall he be called.*   Isa. 54:4-5

In this promise to Israel, and through her to the Church, Jehovah promises to remove their shame and *even the memory of it*. Significantly five different Hebrew words are each rendered as 'shame' in Isaiah 54, and are used to describe that which He will remove from them. Five is the Hebrew number for 'grace.' God's will is for His people and those called by His Name to be freed from every kind of shame.

It is His will is for you to be free from every taint of shame!

Self-Reformation Will Not Do the Job
Trying to change or to 'clean up your act' is an enviable goal, but will not get the job done. You will need to repent and confess the sins involved, and seek the Lord for deliverance from the shame which has entered your life.

The keys to victory over shame are the same as those for seeking freedom in other areas. They are:

Confession
Repentance
Forgiveness
Deliverance

Knowing the Truth

Simply knowing the truth that sets you free is not sufficient. One must experience it, which means it must make the transition from head-knowledge to heart-knowledge. There is 'believing with the mind' and 'believing with the heart,' and there is a great difference in these two kinds of knowing. A minister friend used to say, "The greatest distance in the world is the eighteen inches between your head and your heart."

It is one thing to know something in your mind. and it is entirely different to believe it in your heart. This is exemplified in the miraculous work of forgiveness which we witness so often. We see it at work when a person believes that he has done something too terrible to be forgiven, only to then hear the truth that God loves him in spite of what he has done, and that God is willing to forgive him if he will but repent. What a marvelous transformation occurs when that transition from head-knowledge to heart-knowledge takes place, and we realize that we are forgiven and loved!

The keys to victory from shame, which are similar to those for seeking freedom in other areas, are listed on the following page, and then are presented in seven more detailed steps:

The Seven Steps to Freedom from Shame

1. Confession

Confess to eliminate all roots of guilt.

* Confess every known or suspected area of guilt; all sins of which you are aware.
* Confess your faults one to another, with a prayer partner or deliverance minister

Confess your faults one to another, and pray one for another, that ye may be healed.

James 5:16a

To profess your confession, you might want to use a simple prayer such as the following:

Father, I now confess before You every unconfessed sin that I am aware of, especially _____, _____, and _____. I am truly sorry that I ever did those things. Please forgive me completely.   *Amen*

2. Discernment

Pray for self-discernment and to be reminded of any person who may have wronged you. Pray for the Holy Spirit to search your heart.

The heart is deceitful above all things, and desperately wicked: who can know it?   Jer. 17:9

You might pray:

Lord, please search me and try me, reveal to me all my shortcomings, so that I may repent of them and become righteous before You.   *Amen*

 The second part of this truth involves the latter part of the verse above from James: pray for other brothers and sisters in the Lord, just as you want them to pray for you.

3. **Forgiveness**

Forgive every person whom you feel may have wronged or hurt you.

Unforgiveness is another often overlooked area of sin. Remember the wicked servant: unforgiveness gives the *tormentors* a legal right to attack.

> *And his lord was wroth, and delivered him to the tormentors, till he should pay all that was due unto him. So likewise shall my heavenly Father do also unto you, if ye from your hearts forgive not every one his brother their trespasses.*   Mat. 18:34-35

> *Bless them that curse you, and pray for them which despitefully use you.*   Luke 6:28

You might want to pray a prayer like this:

Lord Jesus, I forgive each of the following people whom I feel have hurt or wronged me in the past, _____, _____, and _____. I ask You to forgive them even as I want You to forgive me.
                              Amen

4. **Repentance**

Repent, not only of every known sin, but also of every area of known or unknown **disobedience** to the Lord, His Word, His will or directions for your life.

> *As many as I love, I rebuke and chasten: be zealous therefore, and repent.* Rev. 3:19

You might want to use a prayer such as the following:

Father, I come to you now to confessing and repenting of everything I have done that has not been righteous and in accordance with your will or your Word.

Amen

5. **Love**

Love your enemies and all men, insofar as you are capable, especially those of the household of God.

Follow God's example and admonition to walk in His way of obedience and love.

> *Be ye therefore followers of God, as dear children; And walk in love, as Christ also hath loved us, and hath given himself for us an offering and a sacrifice to God for a sweetsmelling savour.* Eph. 5:1-2a

> *By this shall all men know that ye are my disciples, if ye have love one to another.* John 13:35

This is my commandment, That ye love one another,
as I have loved you.   John 15:12

6. Deliver Yourself From All Related Spirits

Cast out every evil spirit, whose presence you suspect, especially the spirit of timidity. Command them to leave.

You might use a simple prayer of command such as the following:

I take authority over the spirits tormenting me, especially the shame spirits relating to_____ and _____.
I bind you spirits, of _____ and _____ and I command you to leave me right now in Jesus' name.
                                                Amen

7. Ask God

Ask God for boldness, following the disciple's example:

And now, Lord, behold their threatenings: and grant
*unto thy servants, that with all **boldness** they may speak*
thy word, By stretching forth thine hand to heal; and
that signs and wonders may be done by the name of
thy holy child Jesus. And when they had prayed, the
place was shaken where they were assembled to-
gether; and they were all filled with the Holy Ghost,
*and they spake the word of God with **boldness.***
                                        Acts 4:29-31

Finally, let's deal with the **root of shame**. Let's get rid of your shame now, in the same way that you got rid of your sin, by giving it to Jesus. Pray with me:

Lord Jesus, I confess that I have borne the shame of _____, and_____. I give that shame to you now, for I repent of any and all sins that I have committed which led to this shame, or gave the enemy an opening in my life to permit him to torment me. I renounce all involvement upon my part with every work of darkness, and I ask you now to forgive me and to take away every vestige of shame. For my part, I command the spirits of shame related to_____, _____, and _____, to depart from me now in Jesus' mighty Name!

Amen

Jesus would now say unto you, **"Get your hands off My shame! You have asked me to take your shame, and I have done so. That shame is no longer yours, it is now My shame – I have paid for it."**

Because this is true, your shame is no longer *your* shame, any more than your sins are any longer *your* sins, once you have given them to Jesus.

In Conclusion

The evidence of our deliverance from shame is our ability to bear "reproach" for the sake of the gospel.

Yet if any man suffer as a Christian, let him not be ***ashamed****; but let him glorify God on this behalf.*

1 Pet. 4:16

And they departed from the presence of the council, rejoicing that they were counted worthy to suffer **shame** [disgrace] *for his name.*

Acts 5:41

There are times when being shamed may not be all that bad. In fact, on this occasion, the Apostles were imprisoned and beaten because they had *healed a multitude of sick people, and them which were vexed with unclean spirits.* As a result, the chastened Apostles *rejoiced*, because they had suffered disgrace for His name's sake. We discover, thus, an important truth: that when we have on the armor of righteousness and are shamed or disgraced, it doesn't bother us. On the contrary, **we are blessed!**

Blessed are ye, when men shall revile you, and persecute you, and shall say all manner of evil against you falsely, for my sake.   Mat. 5:11

Blessed are ye, when men shall hate you, and when they shall separate you from their company, and shall reproach you, and cast out your name as evil, for the Son of man's sake.   Luke 6:22

Remember the words of Paul in Hebrews:

For the bodies of those beasts, whose blood is brought into the sanctuary by the high priest for sin, are burned without the camp. Wherefore Jesus also, that he might sanctify the people with his own blood, suffered without the gate. Let us go forth therefore unto him without the camp, bearing his reproach. For here have we no continuing city, but we seek one to come. By him therefore let us offer the sacrifice of praise to God

*continually, that is, the fruit of our lips giving thanks
to his name.*   Heb. 13:11-15

Final Words on Shame

The opposite of shame is glory. Just as Jesus traded shame for eternal glory, so God has promised that we will one day share in His magnificent glory. And the Lord has made it abundantly clear that He wills for us to be *shame-free*, today, in this life.

APPENDIX: I
Hebrew Definitions of
Certain Words Rendered as Shame
From *Strong's Exhaustive Concordance of the Bible*
(Listed in order of appearance in this text, by *Strong's* #)

Hebrew

954. *buwsh, boosh*; a prim. root; prop. to pale, i.e. by impl. to be ashamed; also (by impl.) to be disappointed, or delayed:--(be, make, bring to, cause, put to, with, a-) shame (-d), be (put to) confounded (-fusion), become dry, delay, be long.

8103. *shimtsah, shim-tsaw'*; scornful whispering (of hostile spectators):--shame.

3637. *kalam, kaw-lawm'*; a prim. root; prop. to wound; but only fig., to taunt or insult:--be (make) ashamed, blush, be confounded...(do, put to) shame.

2781. *cherpah, kher-paw'*; from H2778; contumely, disgrace, the pudenda:--rebuke, reproach (-fully), shame."

1322. *bosheth, bo'-sheth*; from H954; shame (the feeling and the condition, as well as its cause); by impl. (spec.) an idol:--ashamed, confusion, + greatly, (put to) shame (-ful thing).

3665. *kana', kaw-nah'*; to bend the knee; hence to humiliate, vanquish: --bring down (low), into subjection, under, humble (self), subdue.

3639. *kelimmah, kel-im-maw'*; from H3637; disgrace: --confusion, dishonour, reproach, shame.

105

8074. *shamem, shaw-mame'*; a prim. root; to stun (or intrans. grow numb), i.e. devastate or (fig.) stupefy (both usually in a passive sense):

2659. *chapher, khaw-fare'*; a prim. root [perh. rath. the same as H2658 through the idea of **detection**]; to blush; fig. to be ashamed, disappointed; causat. to shame, reproach:--be ashamed, be confounded, be brought to confusion (unto shame), come (be put to) shame, bring reproach.

7036. *qalown, kaw-lone';* from H7034; disgrace; (by impl.) the pudenda:--confusion, dishonour, ignominy, reproach, shame.

2616. *chacad, khaw-sad'*; a prim. root; prop. perh. to bow (the neck only [comp. H2603] in courtesy to an equal), i.e. to be kind; also (by euphem. [comp. H1288], but rarely) to reprove:--shew self merciful, put to shame.

6172. 'ervah, er-vaw'; from H6168; nudity, lit. (espec. the pudenda) or fig. (disgrace, blemish):--nakedness, shame, unclean (-ness).

APPENDIX: II
Definitions of Certain Key Words Related to Shame
From *Webster's New World Dictionary*

Ashamed 1. feeling shame because something bad, wrong, or foolish was done 2. feeling humiliated, or embarrassed, as from a sense of inadequacy or inferiority 3. reluctant because feeling shame beforehand

Bashful 1. Very or excessively modest; shy; diffident; retiring. (Implies an instinctive shrinking from public notice that usually shows in awkward demeanor.)

Blame To speak evil of, rooted in Latin word for blaspheme 1. to accuse of being at fault; condemn (*for something*) censure 2. To find fault with (*for something*) 3. To put the responsibility of, as an error, fault, etc., (*on someone or something*) n. 1. the act of blaming; accusation; condemnation; censure 2. Responsibility for a fault or wrong

Blush 1. To become red, esp. in the cheeks or face, as from shame, modesty, or confusion; to flush. 3. To feel shame

Criticism 1. The act of making judgements; analysis of qualities and evaluation of comparative worth... 3. the act of finding fault; censuring; disapproval

Criticize 1. To analyze and judge as a critic 2. To judge disapprovingly; find fault (with); censure

Embarrass Comes from a French root meaning to bar or impede 1. To feel self-conscious, confused, and ill at ease, disconcert, fluster 2. To cause difficulties to; hinder, impede.

107

Guilt 1.a. the act or state of having done a wrong or committed an offense; culpability, legal or ethical b.) a painful feeling of self-reproach resulting from a belief that one has done something wrong or immoral 2. Conduct that involves guilt, crime, sin.

Guilty 1. Having guilt; deserving blame or punishment; culpable 2. having one's guilt proved; legally judged an offender 3. showing or conscious of guilt (*a guilty look*) 4. of or involving guilt or a sense of guilt (*a guilty conscience*).

Rejection / reject To throw or fling back 1. To refuse to take, agree to...., 2. To discard or throw out as worthless, useless, or substandard; cast off or out 3. To pass over or skip..., 5. to rebuff, esp. to deny acceptance, care, love etc., (to someone)*[a rejected child]*

Shame 1.) A painful feeling of having lost the respect of others because of improper behavior, incompetence, etc., of one's self or another 2,) a tendency to have feelings of this kind or a capacity for such feelings 3.) dishonor or disgrace (to bring *shame* to one's family)." The College Edition describes it as: "A painful emotion excited by a consciousness of guilt, shortcomings, or impropriety"; or. "Susceptibility to such feeling or emotion."

Shy 1.Easily frightened; timid 2. Disposed to avoid a person or thing through caution or timidity; distrustful; wary 3. Reserved; bashful. (Implies a shrinking from familiarity or contact with others.)

APPENDIX: III
Clarifications of Meanings:

Ashamed implies embarrassment and sometime guilt felt because of one's own or another's wrong or foolish behavior (*ashamed of his tears*)

Abash implies a sudden loss of self-confidence and a growing feeling of shame or inadequacy (I stood *abashed* at his rebuke),

Censure implies the expression of severe criticism or disapproval by a person in authority or in a position to pass judgment.

Chagrined suggests embarrassment coupled with irritation or regret over what might have been prevented (*chagrined at his error*)

Condemn implies an emphatic pronouncement of blame or guilt, suggesting the rendering of a judicial decision

Embarrassment is to cause to feel ill at ease, so as to result in a loss of composure (*embarrassed* by their compliments);

Humiliated implies a sense of being humbled or disgraced (*humiliated by my failure*) Opposite of proud

Mortified suggests humiliation so great as to seem almost fatal to one's pride or self-esteem (*she was mortified by his obscenities*)

DELIVERANCE FROM FAT & EATING DISORDERS

◆ Why have so many so often failed to lose unwanted weight?

◆ Can weight gain sometimes truly be *unnatural?*

◆ Could Anorexia Nervosa which is basically suicide by starvation, have spiritual roots?

◆ Might Bulimia, compulsive eating and food addictions have a common basis?

◆ What is the "Little Girl Spirit," and what role does it play in Bulimia?

In addition to answering the above questions, more than 80 causes for overeating are disclosed. The author clearly shows that there are many unsuspected roots and sources for overweight conditions. Most overweight people really have no idea as to why they overeat, and often live in continual condemnation for not having sufficient will power or self discipline to control their weight. Many either feel rejected, or that they are unattractive.   **$5.95**

Are you aware that demonic spirits can prevent childbirth...?

DELIVERANCE FROM CHILDLESSNESS

This book offers the first real hope for certain childless couples, because for some, there is a spiritual rather than a physical block preventing conception.

The testimonies included will build your faith as will the Scriptural truths revealed. You will also learn:

✿ HOW CURSES OF CHILDLESSNESS COME INTO BEING, AND HOW THEY MAY BE BROKEN.

✿ WAYS THAT SPIRITS OF INFERTILITY AND STERILITY ENTER, AND HOW TO CAST THEM OUT.

In the first year of publication eight women who had been told they were incapable of having children, advised us that they had *become pregnant after reading this book.*   **$5.95**

WHAT'S BOTHERING YOUR CHILD???

The Little Skunk might save you thousands of dollars...
and years of heartache!

    The Little Skunk is a children's book with a good story
and four-color illustrations, but with a difference: it is
designed as a ministry tool for parents to help their children
talk about what is bothering them!
    This book can be used effectively, even by those with no
understanding of deliverance, and provides a powerful tool
for the skilled minister.
    Since it is intended as a child's introduction to deliver-
ance...there are no scary words. The subjects of demons and
deliverance are not even mentioned in the children's story
portion of the book.

*(Includes instructions for parents on how to best
utilize the book to help their children.)*

The Little Skunk   089228-120-0 Hardback $10.99

DELIVERANCE FOR CHILDREN & TEENS

The first practical handbook for ministering deliverance to children.

The material in this book is arranged to help parents in diagnosing their children's problems and in finding solutions for destructive behavior patterns.

The **Doorways** section of this book illustrates how demons enter, and how they take advantage of innocent, vulnerable children. More than a dozen categories of routes of entry are identified, and examples given!

The section on **Discipline** will be especially helpful to parents who wish to avoid problems, or remove them before they can become entrenched.

The **Mechanics of Ministry** section will help you, step by step, in ministering to a child needing help.

You will learn simple, surprising truths. For example...
* Easiest of all ministry is to small children! * Discipline is the most basic form of spiritual warfare and can bring deliverance!
* A child can acquire demonic problems through heredity or personal experience! * Deliverance need not be frightening if properly presented!

$6.95, Plus $1.75 Shipping

POWERFUL NEW BOOK

This new book is unique because it offers real help for the suffering women who have already had abortions. This book is full of GOOD NEWS!

It shows how to minister to them, or may be used by the women themselves as it contains simple steps to self-ministry.

Millions of women **have had abortions**: every one of them is a potential candidate for the type of ministry presented in this book. Every minister, every counsellor, every Christian should be familiar with these truths which can set people free.

$5.95 + $1.75 Shipping/Handling

Impact Christian Books, Inc.
332 Leffingwell Avenue, Suite 101
Kirkwood, MO 63122

The
Acts
of
Pilate

ANCIENT RECORDS RECORDED BY
CONTEMPORARIES OF JESUS CHRIST
REGARDING THE FACTS CONCERNING
HIS BIRTH, DEATH, RESURRECTION

◆

TRANSLATED FROM THE ORIGINAL LANGUAGES
BY DRS. MCINTOSH and TWOMAN

◆

EDITED BY REV. W.D. MAHAN

This book was a favorite of the late Kathryn Kuhlman who often read from it on her radio show.

Early Church Writers such as Justin refer to the existence of these records, and Tertullian specifically mentions the report made by Pilate to the Emperor of Rome, Tiberius Caesar.

Chapters Include:
◆ *How These Records Were Discovered,*
◆ *A Short Sketch of the Talmuds,*
◆ *Constantine's Letter in Regard to Having Fifty Copies of the Scriptures Written and Bound,*
◆ *Jonathan's Interview with the Bethlehem Shepherds   Letter of Melker, Priest of the Synagogue at Bethlehem,*
◆ *Gamaliel's Interview with Joseph and Mary and Others Concerning Jesus,*
◆ *Report of Caiaphas to the Sanhedrim Concerning the Resurrection of Jesus,*
◆ *Valleus's Notes — "Acta Pilati," or Pilate's Report to Caesar of the Arrest, Trial, and Crucifixion of Jesus,*
◆ *Herod Antipater's Defense Before the Roman Senate in Regard to His Conduct At Bethlehem,*
◆ *Herod Antipas's Defense Before the Roman Senate in Regard to the Execution of John the Baptist,*
◆ *The Hillel Letters Regarding God's Providence to the Jews, by Hillel the Third*

THE ACTS OF PILATE $9.95, plus $2.00 Shipping

IMPACT CHRISTIAN BOOKS, INC.
332 Leffingwell Ave., Suite 101, Kirkwood, MO 63122

Impact Christian Books

332 Leffingwell Ave., Suite 101
Kirkwood, MO 63122

AVAILABLE AT YOUR LOCAL BOOKSTORE, OR YOU MAY
ORDER DIRECTLY. Toll-Free, order-line only M/C, DISC,
or VISA 1-800-451-2708.

Visit our Website at *www. impactchristianbooks.com*

Write for *FREE* Catalog.